REACHING
TOWARD GOD

REFLECTIONS AND EXERCISES
FOR SPIRITUAL GROWTH

Dear Marilyn,

I sure give you a lot of — this is to
meditation reading. This is to
thank you for being so flexible it looks
during the WAIT! I'm sorry it looks
like it will be the last week of school!
I hope you enjoy the book — fun is really
cousin and you know the references on
p. 66 to "the girls" and "girl tots" on p. 59.

Gratefully,
Elli
12/15/97

REACHING TOWARD GOD

REFLECTIONS AND EXERCISES FOR SPIRITUAL GROWTH

JAMES TORRENS, S.J.

SHEED & WARD
KANSAS CITY

Sheed & Ward™ is a service of The National Catholic Reporter Publishing Company.

Library of Congress Cataloguing-in-Publication Data
Torrens, James, 1930-
    Reaching toward God : reflections and exercises for spiritual growth / James Torrens.
        p.   cm.
    ISBN: 1-55612-988-2 (pbk. : alk. paper)
    1. Spirituality–Catholic Church. 2. Catholic Church–Doctrines.
I. Title.
BX2350.2.T662 1997
248.4'82–dc21   97-29757
                                                               CIP

Published by: Sheed & Ward
                 115 E. Armour Blvd.
                 P.O. Box 419492
                 Kansas City, MO 64141-6492

To order, call: (800) 333-7373

www.natcath.com/sheedward

Cover design by James F. Brisson.

CONTENTS

PREFACE

Reaching toward God – it is what we do essentially, it is the dynamic of our life at any age. Even at our darkest, we have an impulse like plants toward the light, an impulse that the poet Theodore Roethke captured in his poem "Root Cellar": "Nothing would sleep in that cellar, dank as a ditch, / Bulbs broke out of boxes hunting for chinks in the dark." We are like that toward God.

Or say we are children with arms flung out to our source expectantly, or pilgrims with arms uplifted, as Virgil put it, "for love of the further shore" (*Aeneid*, bk. 6). To thwart this process, we have to do violence to ourselves – propose false lights and wrench our growth into a wrong direction. Sad to say, we get good at that.

There is, to be sure, something paradoxical about reaching toward God. We never quite attain. *Deus semper major*, God is always beyond. Our achievement of any union is incomplete. We can proceed not one inch of the way without invitation. As Saint Anselm says: "I cannot find you unless you show yourself to me." Yet we know the invitation stays open, and pray with Saint Augustine: "Give me the strength to seek, you who have caused me to find you, and have given me the hope of finding you more and more."

The drama of growing toward God, along with the puzzling and struggling that we do at any stage of the way, is the concern of this book. It contains essays accompanied by poems. They were written over a sixteen-year period for

Human Development, a quarterly magazine under Jesuit sponsorship that links spiritual growth to the achievement of maturity.

Human Development and its editors have based themselves on a theory of human growth by stages, as sketched out by the likes of Jean Piaget, Erik Erikson, Abraham Maslow, Lawrence Kohlberg, Daniel Levinson, and Gail Sheehy. Truth to tell, the insight was recorded long ago in the *Rhetoric* of Aristotle and, during the Renaissance, in the speech by Jacques in Shakespeare's *As You Like It* about the seven stages of life (act 2, scene 7).

The author's bent in these pages is literary and classical, so his approach owes more, no doubt, to Shakespeare and Aristotle than to the psychologists of our century. Psychology, however, has posed a host of questions to the spiritual concepts I grew up with – self-denial, suppression of pride, custody of the eyes (and modesty and angelic purity), contempt of the world, detachment, fervor of devotion, turning the other cheek, unflagging zeal, mortification.

There is no question – not to me, at least – of junking the ancient wisdom. "Mortification," for instance, is the linchpin of Jesuit spirituality. Saint Ignatius Loyola used this norm to judge whether a given person, touted as holy, was indeed authentic as a follower of Christ or just putting on a good show. For him "mortification" meant something quite other than the capacity for spectacular fasts and drawn-out prayer, though he had been capable of these. It implied a more than ordinary self-knowledge, docility to the Holy Spirit, and clarity of purpose.

These days a conversation has to go on between the high demands of Christian faith, its generous impulses, and contemporary insights on mental health and personal growth, such as burnout, self-esteem, assertiveness, and mature sexuality. That is what these essays try to do, focusing upon a subject area such as aging or leisure or proposing a particular slant. I hope these essays lead toward what we call these days "integration." I also hope that each chapter spurs reflection and debate among readers. For this purpose, each chapter concludes with a section called "Reflection and Action," by which the reader can digest and personalize the content. This section encourages journal keeping.

I am grateful, beyond what I can express here, to the editor and founder of *Human Development,* Fr. James Gill, S.J., psychiatrist and teacher, for being so amenable, in the opening year of his publication, to my wild notion of a regular column composed of a poem plus a related essay, and then for sticking with me all the way. I am equally in debt to Linda Amadeo, executive editor, for continual encouragement and for handling my frequent emendations and revisions (the nightmare of editorial staff) without a blink.

I owe quite specific thanks to Daniel Wackerman, assistant editor of *America,* for effecting the passage of all this material from the printed page back into computer files, via that remarkable machine the scanner. This process of rereading and selecting has also allowed me to touch up the poems and essays considerably in the process of publication. Revising and polishing constitute one of the continuing sagas of our life!

CHAPTER ONE

THE PILGRIM JOURNEY

PIECING OUT THE MAP

Here in my own vague reaches,
directions jotted and then
left at home, night-lit,
I'm picking my way through.

You start, nose pointing
where it should, and go
until street names don't
register, landmarks have
whizzed by. Let's turn here,
hoping for a connection.
Dead end. You swing into
a driveway, whirl about.

You drift and squint, cars
honking. You swerve to
a gas pump where the attendant
shrugs, "Sorry, just
started here. Can't help."

Someone does, reeling off
street names, lefts, rights,
"so many stop lights, such and
such a store. Can't miss it."
Which, of course, you do,

lose track, pounding
the dashboard, pooped,
and inch along until
a happy turn, pure chance,
and you are back in grace.

At home out comes the map.
Aha! So that was it!
You piece out your city
bit by bit in your head.
Next time a little more
filled in, if you remember
faster than for sure forget.

Set down in unfamiliar places, some people instinctively find their way. The most haphazard city, with oddly arranged districts and meandering cross streets, is a challenge they seem to relish. Blindfold them, transport them, keep the sun behind clouds – once unblinkered, they point unerringly north.

There are many humans, not all of them politicians, with a genius for sniffing out a situation. They seem to have a sixth sense for discerning who stands in what relationship to whom, and especially who holds the cards. They are the natural survivors, the thrivers.

I am not one of the above. What I find to be habitual is my puzzlement over any new scene, a slow start into new areas of understanding. Give me directions at all complicated, at all out of familiar territory, and the welter of alternatives as I go blurs the indications I have been given. The more assurance I go out with, the more disaster is likely.

Most of us need all the help we can get when venturing into new realms – insurance policies, car maintenance, dieting, child rearing. The same holds true for the really demanding situations, such as living with an addicted, depressed, or badly injured person. Living with ourselves, we round corners into unexpected feelings, impulses, attitudes, quandaries, domestic and professional complications – all of which call for the wisest readings we can elicit.

Our landscapes are so complicated these days. In an office or a shop, on a school campus, in a peer group or an extended family, we find ourselves pondering the people about us. What indeed is happening before our eyes, on people's faces or in their hearts? We strive for fair and accurate assessments, not just convenient or fashionable boxes to put folks in. We do this not to maneuver people or outmaneuver them, not to avoid pain in dealing with them or to avoid looking foolish, but above all to fulfill our responsibility to them, to love and to do justice.

Our lives, so mysterious in origin and destiny, come to us as an unexplored land, a sort of wilderness area into which we are invited to venture and find our way around. In earlier, less detailed times, both world and local maps showed much uncharted terrain. "Darkest Africa" was once the paradigm, although Joseph Conrad corrected this image into a blank space of sheer white in *The Heart of Darkness*. Thoreau, earlier, asked in the conclusion to *Walden*: "Is not our own interior white on the chart?"

Today, as ever, what a tragedy and waste that so many people – elderly, middle-aged, even teenaged – at some imperceptible point decide, "I can manage within this special circle, within these lines. What is outside will have to stay there." Thoreau commented on our penchant for letting outside factors circumscribe us: "We think that if rail fences are pulled down, or stone walls piled up on our farms, bounds are henceforth set to our lives and our fates decided." We think that running out of money for graduate school or having an ailing parent to tend or losing our mobility rules out aspirations.

Willy-nilly, events often force us into action, into being cartographers. We find we have to study some area of medicine or business, learn some technology, tap into accumulated wisdom, try some initiatives. The encouragement comes again from Thoreau: "Be a Columbus to whole new continents and worlds within you, opening new channels not of trade but of thought." For T. S. Eliot it was never too late, as we see from this paradox in the *Four Quartets*: "Old men should be explorers."

We never really finish the process of sketching out our lives. Death merely finds us with whatever map we have managed to draw. But how complex and interesting often. And in rare instances of the highly developed young, with what pure and clean lines! We all fill in, we piece out the map. Time and failing memory may erase, may garble, but we go on groping for the road that mysteriously draws us.

REFLECTION AND ACTION

Preliminary Note:

As you move through these chapters, try to keep a notebook or a journal, extending the chapters or arguing with them for your own benefit.

Food for Thought:

Review in your life the paths you thought you would take that closed off gradually or suddenly. Remember, as well, the times of indecision and fretful weighing of options. How was God dealing with you and how were you responding?

And today, with what mixture of anxiety, peacefulness, or courage do you face the future?

Suggested steps:

Compose a brief prayer about the attitude you wish to face into the future with.

Integrate this prayer into the days ahead.

SHAPE OF A DAY

a day.
it comes fitting you to itself
It wants to wear

This is me, it says,
in patches vivid or dull.
some pieces rub raw. but here, here
exquisite.
Make me look good

or you get long stretches

Have you sat with it in your hands,
official, stiff,
its own field of force?
trouser legs exacting a noble stand
so much comes pale from
waiting rooms, needs color

and the light stuff, flowered
or riding easily if plain,
cut for the neck, airy.
The busiest should not pass these
up

and the fancy cuts. Lord!
worth watching for
goods. stuff.

It takes shape hour by hour,
with a quizzical look.
Don't make me come out wrong,
it pleads. Each nighttime
clearly tells.

How precious a day, a single day! So many of us living dully
or anxiously or even exhaustedly let our days slip by. People
remark, coming off a tedious job, "Well, chalk off another
day." The words breathe relief, but what a waste. A person
feeling this way admits, in effect, "My days unroll one just
like another, in a long string, and I just disposed of one
more." "As if you could kill time," Thoreau said, "without
injuring eternity."

The most precious thing about each day is that you can
give it shape. It begs to be allowed a form. We are not the
prime agents in such a process, for the moments of opportunity or testing that arrive before us are providential. Someone who loves us is providing them. But we alone can detect
their latent shape. This takes us beyond the skill that hand-
books refer to as time management. Not that we should
disdain this skill; we badly need it. But time management is
technique and orderliness, whereas we must aim at art, at
design. And we must capitalize on surprise, like the water
colorist adapting a spilled blob of paint.

The habit of journal keeping, honored in so many
cultures and countries, is a first step in shaping time. Trav-
elers are still the most diligent keepers of journals; they do
not want the impact of a few hours at the Great Wall of
China to be crowded from memory by a later visit to some
model commune or the Forbidden City. We most need,
however, to ponder and shape not the extraordinary but
the ordinary, exercising attentiveness on what seems, decep-
tively, the most familiar and workaday.

I look back with astonishment now on some few of my own spotty journal entries and welcome renewed contact with the moments of grace they keep alive. "June 19. Hard day! I came back from a few days of respite to the burden of all that awaited me back home. It weighed heavily and, I'm afraid, made me snap at a few people. Yet our evening Mass renewed my hopes that the ability to bear, and be, and do, and hardest of all, decide, is conferred by the One who says, 'I will not fail you or desert you.'"

Ignatius of Loyola invented a technique that he called the "examen," proposing it in his *Spiritual Exercises*. Many of us remember it not too fondly in its elementary form in which the beginner is trained to notice and record and eventually weed out one particular fault at a time. The method invites comparison with that project of self-perfection via lined pages and daily notations recommended by Benjamin Franklin in his *Autobiography*. And we remember how D. H. Lawrence derided Franklin's text for the smugness he detected there.

But Ignatius, outlining a life for his companions and insisting that the examen is of central import, clearly meant it to be more than a simple ablution of misdemeanors or a filing-off of rough edges. He instructed his followers that any other form of prayer – meditation, breviary, rosary – can yield to the pressure of duties, but not the examen. Why not? Because this is to be the moment of self-examination when we consider what the day's principal events have been saying to us, how we have responded to them, and whether we have husbanded and dispensed our love well.

The adventure of shaping each of our days, to make the best of its one chance, should start the night before or soon after rising, with attention to some text or context. Most often the Scripture of the day holds as a kernel the motif that will govern what is to transpire. It sounds a theme for our day. It speaks directly to some weak part of us that

needs bolstering, to some rationalization or passion that
needs uncovering, to an opportunity that is going to present
itself. Example. I find myself obsessed every so often by sour
thoughts about an individual, sparked by some minor incident. How embarrassing yet how helpful it was one day when
the following motif, drawn from the morning's gospel,
popped into my head, "You shall not kill" – you shall not
murder your brother in your thoughts. The resolution had
been planted long ahead of the difficulty.

It is uncanny how the day can be pervaded, how a
message can keep resonating. A day's gospel not too long
ago centered on the announcement, "The kingdom of
heaven has drawn near." DeLubac's explanation, drawn
from the Church Fathers, is that Jesus is the kingdom in
person. Remarkably, a number of pastoral or consultative
moments in that day brought these words home, whether
it was sounded through colleagues who were reinforcing the
message to me or through me as I was conveying it to others.

Thus each day is an adventure. We do not live by
months or years or even so much by seasons as we do by
individual days. Hugo Rahner has put it neatly in *Ignatius
the Theologian*: "All times are compressed into 'the present
moment,' into 'today' – for every 'today' can bring salvation,
and it is time when one must hear his voice and not harden
one's heart." His sentence rephrases Psalm 95, with which
each morning's breviary begins.

I myself seem just now to have discovered this potenti-
ality of my days, with half a century of them already gone.
Where can I possibly have been displacing my attention? A
thrill (a terror too) comes from finding how much more
weight and body the time can carry. Miguel de Unamuno,
in *Our Lord Don Quixote*, may be allowed the last word. He
writes the following words in his opening pages, which turn
to Ignatius Loyola for a striking point of comparison with
that undaunted striver Quixote: "The most urgent matter

is the one here and now; in the moment that passes and in the narrow space we occupy lies our eternity and our infinity." The moment passes quickly, no question, and a follower comes, but the moments readily compose. And what they form, the shape they need to take, is a day.

REFLECTION AND ACTION

Food for Thought:
Reflect on the measure of optimism, excitement, sense of adventure – or alas, of their opposite – with which you face each day.

Suggested Steps:
As St. Ignatius proposed, take some time at the end of each day, or even earlier, to consider what the principal events of that day have been saying to you, how you have responded to them, and whether you have nurtured and dispensed your love well.

At the beginning of tomorrow, or just before retiring tonight, read over the liturgical text for tomorrow. What theme or motif does it suggest? Try following out this thread during the day.

REGRESSION IN SERVICE OF THE EGO

Feeding time. Open the book
so the beast can nibble. Nod him back
into his dream cave, or unblock
the city exit into sun. A box
has to let its flaps down, and blithely
out will pop Jack, relieved and blinking,
his tongue rudely out. Don't brusquely
stuff him back in. Friend, if you beckon
the file clerk from his scrabble, with beak
wide he will crow grandly. Unbridle

the workhorse, slipping a grub sack
over his pet nose. "Slow, slow, or you'll burst,
poor creature." He has borne the brunt.
A short space now he relaxes on the brink.

As a live-in faculty member in a Jesuit college dormitory
during the seventies and eighties, I witnessed an astonishing
ritual on the eve of final exams. It was played out between
residence halls in a very tight quad, with a paved square
between them. On the Sunday of hardest study and greatest
anxiety, after the 10 p.m. campus Mass, men of one hall
would gather and begin yelling vigorous insults, ranging
from the clever to the appallingly crude, at the inhabitants
of the facing dorm. They of course answered in kind, the
males cheered on by women in the upper windows. The
tempo built and the barrage got heavier. Then about mid-
night, as if by prearrangement, it all stopped and students
went back quietly to their desks to resume studying.

The Encyclopedia of Psychoanalysis classifies the above
phenomenon as "regression in service of the ego." It runs
according to the textbook – all hell let loose within perime-
ters. Says the *Encyclopedia*: "The essential quality of these
regressions in service of the ego [i.e., of the total personality]
is that they are controlled; they are circumscribed, transient,
and reversible." These college capers are the stuff of storytelling in a later life. Anyone caught in the shoutout, however, finds this "instinctual diffusion," this "influx of
infantile aggressive energies," rather less than charming.

Admittedly our Dionysian face needs to show itself from
time to time; to be too disapproving makes one liable to be
cast as that sour Puritan Malvolio of whom Shakespeare
makes fun in *Twelfth Night*. Still, I cannot help thinking how
typical this event is of the so-called adult world, in which
day-and-night attention to business, politics, medicine,
graduate studies, a cause, or a movement, takes its punishing

toll, building up pressure toward the episode of release, the decontrol of instincts, or the hiatus of responsibility. Idealists are as subject as anyone else to this dynamic, which Freudians interpret as a damming up of instincts with inevitable chaotic outburst. Compulsive work followed by hell-bent recreation – that is surely one of the "diseases of civilization."

To mature – or just to age – is to recognize oneself as flesh and blood, with flow and reflux of energies. And who, at whatever age, does not need to breathe normally, to hit one's own pace even when kept on the run? Our individual gifts come with built-in specifications: Use for a given period, in this particular way, to the following ends.

We are all subject to the awesome rhythm described in the book of Ecclesiastes: "For everything there is a season, and a time for every matter under heaven." To paraphrase: There is a time to be on stage and a time to slouch in the loge; a time for talking turkey, a time to bite one's lip, and a time for just chatting; a time to push Brother Ass, as St. Francis would say, and a time to let him rest. But we also need to spell out what other ages took for granted, that a rhythm is not an oscillation between extremes. The life that looks like jagged lightning strokes when plotted on a chart cannot be called "rhythmic."

The law of Moses contains as its third major precept the rule of sabbath observance, that there be a fallow time for the earth and a rest period for the arms and brain to help us enter into God's fruitful repose. Pay God the tribute of admitting that you are a creature – that is what the law says. To circumvent the clever hedging and dodging of humans, interpreters spelled out sabbath observance in minute details that soon became onerous. The heart of the commandment got lost, and it still is. The busiest and most idealistic people show themselves most adept at screening out this question: How should the spirit of the Third Commandment help me shape the Lord's Day?

The spirit of the Third Commandment should also nudge us toward some daily order, the determination that a high-pressure day contain its breathing spaces, to say nothing of its prayer times. The creature that we are does not need pampering, the kind of excessive attention that blocks off generosity, but only the humble attentiveness that will keep it healthy and toned for service human and divine. If it is driven bullheadedly, if it is not refreshed and allowed to stop at an occasional oasis (not a pub necessarily!), the creature may have the last word by lapses of performance, by some outburst, by a complete collapse – or perhaps, as Francis Marien, S.J., once observed, it will just psychically poop out.

REFLECTION AND ACTION

Food for Thought:
Describe to yourself the rhythm of your life, whether it is keyed up, perhaps compulsive or just ultrabusy; whether, by contrast, it is on the lethargic side; or whether it achieves some regularity – healthy admixture of busyness, ease, prayer, socializing, and exercise.

As to regression in service of the ego, any of that?

Suggested Steps:
Plot out the balance of elements you would like in a day.

As for the Lord's Day and the Third Commandment, plan some way of keeping it that eases up on work and allows room for God. (Given some people's commitments or schedules of work, the spirit of sabbath may need to fall elsewhere than Sunday.)

COMING TO REASON

Last night, running out of drink,
we took early retirement (vowing
never again), to awaken clear as birds
for once, throw a robe on, light up,
and step outside, coinciding with dawn.

"My God, it's gorgeous!" We knew then
you cannot tell a person things.
The familiar hangs ripening and falls.
You have to be there
catching like Newton with a name.

We locked arms reentering. Our sharp
looks over coffee agreed, Who needs
the hair of the dog! "Funny," she said,
"It hits me, children don't have to
thank." And I, "Late, but our light goes on."

Remember when we used to designate age seven as the age of reason? We still use that age as a rough working norm for First Communion, with our hunch that about this time children become able to grasp some quite serious things. (We also know how restless and full of beans they can still be.) We know, on the other hand, that quite mysteriously, the reasoning power, tremendous and not to be underestimated, begins to operate at or even before birth. Hence the Eastern Church, the Byzantine Catholic rite, has been giving even tiny children a taste of the Holy Species, along with their parents, because receiving the Eucharist is essentially an exercise of faith, a gift coming to us through the Church.

We all – Eastern and Western, youngish and aging – recognize that to become reasonable takes a lifetime and then some. This recognition, which is already a step far along in the process of maturing, makes us humble recipients of the gifts of the Spirit when they come. Here again, we can hardly underestimate the powers given us on the occasion of our second birth, the outpouring of the Lord's Spirit on us in baptism, as a result of which we are rooted in true goodness, given an unerring direction toward the fullness of Christ, and made subject daily to forces of transformation from within.

And yet, far from solving everything, our baptism, our identification with Christ, often makes more glaring the gap between what we are meant or supposed to be and what we actually are. St. Paul addressed the Corinthians as a "holy people of Jesus Christ, who are called to take their place among all the saints everywhere" (1 Cor 1:2). He was not flattering them or being ironic. It was what he found most true – this despite also finding them childishly competing other churches for prestige and honor, susceptible to the sensuality of a port city, and stingy in supporting the destitute Jewish Christians back in the Holy Land. He was trying to lead them on from being milk-fed Christians to being mature.

What a big order! How long it takes for almost everyone! These days late in the twentieth century give us the frequent spectacle of people coming to their senses, beginning to straighten out, far along the road of their lives. Second careers often mean that people find themselves first after painfully switching direction; so do some second marriages or the return to secular life from religious orders. Considering the fallout, the hurt to others, and the occasional wreckage that the second chance often entails, it does not, as a solution, satisfy as fully as the rediscovery of a first love. But it is a solution, often the only one; sometimes it is the originally right one reasserting itself.

A person should be happy and feel privileged, no matter how late in life to gain some stability, to learn to give and take, to "mellow out." The Catholic Church, in its approach to dispensations and annulments, has come, if slowly, to recognize this, even while struggling to keep the sights clear and not to play fast and loose with serious commitments.

The people who come to reason late, very late, are often terribly accomplished in business or professions – masters of computer systems, skilled repairpersons, tenders of others, clever arrangers of anything under the sun. They prove deficient in just one thing: self-possession (which, paradoxically involves relinquishing the self). To come to understand what we are truly like and who, as individuals before God, we truly are, and what is the potential or gift still locked up in us happens at a much different rhythm from learning to use a computer or mastering a system of accounting. It is a matter of both swallowing the hard truths and daring to believe the redemptive ones – the two sides of our salvation.

The redeeming truths are those gifts of birth without which we would not be at all (or be particularly skilled) and those baptismal gifts without which we would be lost. Often we do not dare even admit them to ourselves, because we might have to take some big steps, possibly change our whole orientation. For example, suppose we are working under oppressive management, which we put up with and we shut up about because we like what we ourselves are doing and do not want to be stomped. But our very dignity calls sometimes for a courageous move. The Karen Silkwood story, the movie *Silkwood*, is about that – an imperfect woman upon whom it dawned one day that to live well she had to take a dangerous initiative. What helped her was the realization that life itself, her life, was already brimful of danger.

The poet Rilke has a marvelous sonnet about the Archaic Torso of Apollo, the enormous twisting trunk that thousands have viewed along with the smooth Apollo Belvedere in the Vatican Art Exhibit. The body itself, Rilke says to his reader, is full of gleams, expressions, and communications to you if you dare look at it, which are summed up in the sonnet's final words: "You must change your lives." Just such an effect should the body of our faith have on us.

As to the hard truths, these emerge after some sharp questions. What is it in us that causes pain to others, our conscious or only half-realized patterns that needlessly and often cause difficulties or distress? Or, taking another tack, what way of acting and thinking is self-destructive for us? Are we carrying some resentment night and day? Are we too keen always to have someone else think well of us? Are we anxious for security beyond all readiness to risk? These are lapses of faith or charity possible to the baptized wherein the Holy Spirit is hindered from filling us.

How indeed are we to grow? The poet Dante in his long epic of pilgrimage to God, *The Divine Comedy,* exploited the image of a climb up Mount Purgatory. The climbers wind around with some sense of give and stretch and leisurely pace in the effort, but they follow basically a spiral upward. They meet numerous others who, even amid pain, are happy to be reshaping themselves, redirecting their love.

T. S. Eliot in "Ash Wednesday" (1928) retouches this notion of Dante's. He pictures our growth as movement up a winding stair with pauses at various turnings, either to look down with a shudder on times of trouble and temptation glimpsed below or to look out a narrow window at romantic images from the past with hankering, but with a sense that they are beyond recovery. Eliot sees old age and difficulty above, but also the entry into God. Dante finds at the mountaintop the Earthly Paradise, a return to innocence, the discovery of love in its true condition, God coming to us in those we love.

Blessed are those who do come to reason, even if late. More blessed, those so guided from the start. The Church works with couples who have stated an intention to marry, to assess them and also to help them develop understanding and true commitment. Those most in need of help, perhaps, are at the other end of the process, those for whom things seem to come unstuck just when they should be firming up. Issues beset them – desires, fears, resentments – with which they have never really dealt. They get the terrible sensation of going downhill rather than up.

But this time of shaking can also be a time of illumination. Healing attitudes or memories can be evoked, receptiveness to God's surprises and providential signs. Strategies may be undertaken to help us respond, but mostly a new kind of honesty with ourselves, and a humble look to the Other. Opportunity does not always dress up when it comes. "In a dark time," wrote the poet Theodore Roethke, who had endured many of them, "the eye begins to see."

The most sophisticated charts of our maturing process, for example, the steps to moral insight as charted by Kohlberg and retouched by Carol Gilligan, are at best inspired generalities. They fit individual cases, but with much pushing and shoving. God's times and seasons – ours, looked at from the truly large view – are unpredictable. The goal remains the same: arriving at "the mature human state, the growth mark of the fullness of Christ" (Eph 4:13). But how slow our arriving; what a long time we take, with so much untwisting and redirecting and so many new starts in coming to reason. We welcome to any strong indications that we are already doing so!

REFLECTION AND ACTION

Food for Thought:

Reflect on some experience of "coming to reason," some access of maturity in your own life.

This project of achieving "the growth mark of the fullness of Christ" suffers many hesitations and reversals, and depends heavily on the Holy Spirit. Can you trace it, to some degree?

Suggested Steps:

Step beyond strong regrets or resentments that you may still nurture. This may have to take place principally within the memory and personal attitudes, but perhaps it will also call for external steps. Composing a prayer would help achieve a proper orientation.

MOSTLY IT TAKES YEARS

Mostly it takes us years
and second chances to untwist,
relax our faces, admit to someone
"Sorry" about some old thing.
Years to come out well.
Like the desert plant nobody has seen
bloom ever, but the expert says
"Wait" and one day, Surprise!
it unfolds brilliantly. And what a
fragrance! Mostly it takes years.

My mother in her eighty-sixth year has lost none of her sharp interest in the world around her and still utters her gratitude for each day granted her. Still, she has pointed out to me more than once, "Jim, it's hard to be old." To watch her at this stage and to attend to her makes me conscious of my own life, all of our lives, slipping away. Just beyond the peak the road winds downhill. So, at least, we are tempted to think.

Tom Eliot, an undergraduate at Harvard circa 1914, conjured up in poetry a young adult named J. Alfred Prufrock, already in a rut, the fires of initiative already banked. "I grow old, I grow old," this character complains. I had better do something daring, he thinks; "I shall wear the bottom of my trousers rolled." He frets about his appearance and figure, painfully self-conscious: "Shall I part my hair behind? Do I dare to eat a peach?" And as to the mermaids, the young ladies, well, I'm balding and not up to date; "I do not think that they will sing to me."

Eliot's lines are still up-to-date. Some people stand around regretting lost youth; we call it depression. Others push themselves to prove they haven't lost it. Meanwhile America practices its cult of youthfulness – its celebration of frantic energy, its favoritism for hotshot young executives and technicians, its cosmetology. This is all a denial of death. Rather than accepting our natural condition and looking to it as a gateway, we fear death and are obsessed with it.

Rilke the poet, in his *Duino Elegies* and *Sonnets to Orpheus*, looked at death as a realm continually interpenetrating with life, sending its angels to us and receiving us. We who receive the Eucharist often do not always recall that this bread of immortality, the body of Jesus risen, makes us participants in another realm.

The evidence of what Teilhard de Chardin called our "passivities of diminishment," aging as a process always underway, need not be a fright. So much depends on how we receive gifts, the ones that come when we are hoping for something else: the loss of friends, vigor, glamour, sharp senses, or memory; the loss also of some ground or status as a professional or a careerwoman, as a housemother or a kingpin. Such reminders of mortality drive people at all stages, perhaps especially those in the last stage, to tranquil-

izers and sedatives and often to the liquor store. How sad
that our advanced society has life so wrong, that it fosters
in people somehow the fear of becoming discards.

Father Hans von Balthasar has some moving words
from a different perspective in *Heart of the World*. Time, he
says, unwraps our fingers from whatever we clutch, teaching
us to give ourselves away and showing us to Whom:

> In one and the same act He clothes you out of love and
> strips you out of love; He presses all treasures into your
> hand and the most precious jewel of all, to love Him in
> return; and nevertheless again takes away everything He
> has given so that you love not the gift but the giver, and
> so that you know, even in giving, that you are but a wave
> in His stream.

The most encouraging people on this planet seem to
fall into two classes, those flinging themselves and their
energies into some heroic human service and those who
grow old gracefully. Jesus did not have a chance to grow
old. Or did he, full of wisdom and grace, as he showed
himself from the start? Although the embittered elderly are
a terror (a sadness rather, if we really understood), the
weathered face with the glad spark and the direct contemplative interest cheers everyone.

The key seems to be our concept of maturity. Maturity
– readiness for the picking! Length of life comes as a special
providence for many of us – we are such slow learners! It
takes so long to learn unpossessive love, anger that can go
down with the sun, forgiveness that is not just the mark of
a patsy, inventiveness that will cheer the gloomy, and understanding God's closeness and ways. These are the habits
that help a person shape events rather than cower before
them.

This is the wisdom that the Chinese, the Africans, and
so many others attribute to grandparents and elders. We
should not make wrong claims on its behalf, for none of us

is easily fooled. That vaunted experience of the elderly can seem shaky indeed with the world changing at such a rate and all fields of endeavor so hard to keep up with. Even self-understanding, in the course of what T. S. Eliot called "the rendering pain of re-enactment of all that you have done, and been," is so elusive.

Hence Eliot, in the great poem of his later years, "Four Quartets," which addresses aging as an opportunity for redeeming time, made a difficult point: "Do not let me hear of the wisdom of old men. . . . The only wisdom we can hope to acquire is the wisdom of humility." Yet this humility is the very opposite of learned helplessness, which afflicts so many in nursing homes. In our profound awareness of that paralytic state wherein we are lowered continually before the Divine, we know with what life he graces and fills us unto the end.

Fortunately, diminishing expertise, drive, or physical sharpness does not have to mean loss of interest. Quite the contrary in these days of continuing education and second and third careers, as fostered by various enterprises of adult learning. I am familiar, in particular, with the Fromm Institute at the University of San Francisco; but the best known and most widely attended seems at the moment to be Elderhostel. Nor do we lose the accumulations of our history. Lee Cobb, when called toward the end of his life to act King Lear in a New York production, admitted that it had been a lifelong ambition of his to play this part. He explained why: "Because the old are so much more interesting than anyone else; so much more has happened to them." And they are still such resources. In my Jesuit university community, the best classicists, the best Church historians, the best social activists, and the best-read individuals are, right now, the retired people.

According to Anne Marie Kaune in *The Catholic Worker* (October/November 1981), it was only with reluctance that

Dorothy Day referred to her last few years as her retirement. "She would go on to note that the Buddhists revere old age as the valuable third stage of life, a time of contemplation and deepening in wisdom in preparation for the next life – how much richer than retirement." A Little Brother of the Gospel, Giorgio, remarked: "I am amazed to see how she lived the last years of her life as a poor woman. . . . There was such a light in her eyes, a light from someplace else."

Two decades ago, at the death of Leo Madigan, S.J., this elderly priest noted for his puns and bons mots was found to have left behind him a sheaf of personal notes stretching back for years. Some of Madigan's best sayings, far from being spontaneous, turn out to have been carefully culled from his reading: "live – don't mildew," "purgatory is God's I.C.U."; "bald-headed priest – visible head of the Church." He also had marvelous and very humble reflections on his own state: "I'm going through energy crisis"; "just sitting here doing my spiritual knitting"; "no harder labor than enforced idleness."

Madigan's spiritual insights, kept entirely for himself, are wonderful: "loneliness of retired priests – God's last gift to wean them from applause of friends to Himself"; "instinctively relax in indwelling – intimate commune – instead of books, papers, etc., most profitable and pleasing"; "Lord, make me 'feel at home' with you, filial, intimate, so we won't be strangers at death." And his humor never deserted him: "No one is completely useless. I can at least serve as a horrible example." Horrible, nothing! A person like Madigan never fully departs; even when setting off to God, he continues very much around.

The central task of maturing (progressing to a ripe age), again as Eliot tells it (he learned from Dante), is paradoxically to achieve the innocence of youth. This youth that we sometimes glimpse in the elderly (particularly some nuns) consists of the kind of trust spoken of in Psalm 131:

instinctive humor, closeness to God, simplicity of concerns, and reconcilement (no more paranoia about "them" or bitterness about some "her" or "him"). F. L. Lucas says about that kind of youth: "In real life the finest characters become simpler as their lives draw toward their close – not because they have grown less subtle, but because their values have grown clearer."

We say in amazement about certain people that he or she is really blossoming. This can be said of them at any age, but it generally means there has been some delay in the normal rhythm and indicates a pleasant surprise at a development that more than compensates. Aging as a vocation is precisely the calling to be late bloomers.

REFLECTION AND ACTION

Food for Thought:

As honestly as may be, describe your attitude to growing older, not excluding the matter of self-image but including also the effect aging may have on your present occupation. Indicate too how your faith operates at this level.

Suggested Steps:

Possessiveness mars one's peace. Dispossess, to the extent that this is possible and makes sense.

Strive to keep alive interests and friendships that have nourished you in the past.

Good health and health care is such a major preoccupation these days. Try to be conscious of this topic without forever harping on it.

FOR THOSE WHO GO

> Seeing our friends off
> who mostly hate to go.
> Surface that sails them
> never rounds them back.
>
> Dear ones, so hard
> breaking the embrace.
> Have we an argument
> to settle? Silly! Home's free.
>
> Dark, blessed element
> take you, as one day us.
> We beg of your fixed smile,
> light up and up.

What difficult months these have been! On the second day of school one of my students, age twenty, collapsed and died before the class while reading a humorous account from summer Bible camp, where she had acted as counselor. Because of a work stoppage at the county coroner's, autopsy and analysis took forever to reveal the cause, an aneurysm. Another student, one of my favorites from last year, fell asleep at the wheel while driving home from her sister's wedding and went into a river. The effect of such an event is stunning. Then a Jesuit contemporary of mine, one of those classic helpers and "tracers of lost persons," went off to the Lord in the midst of plans still unachieved. Another, the pioneer of the Summer Theology Program at the University of San Francisco, followed him a week later, after forty years of severe arthritis. Who can take seriously the advice of the poet William Butler Yeats, "Cast a cold eye on life, on death"? He postulates a detachment, a distance, that corresponds very little to our close involvement with those who go from our midst.

Perhaps I am, in fact, more detached from my two students than from my confreres. I am proud of these two, of the humor and eager interest and goodness that graced their lives. With my fellow religious, things are more complicated. Convinced as I was for a long time that there is a classic, pious way of dying – dying by the book, as it were – I now have to admit how often, among those I know well, things do not seem to go that way. Some cling surprisingly hard even while struggling against those who nurse them.

"Denial," the standard, ready explanation, is much too harsh and shallow. After all, we are talking about the strongest natural instinct, the impulse to keep alive – and more than that, to keep our role in an unfolding drama. We are talking also of people who, familiar with this globe of ours and filled with the light of its memories, flinch before the terror of extinction. A cry was wrenched from Jesus as he felt himself being engulfed in darkness. His gesture of trusting self-abandonment in the spirit of the psalms, which St. Luke recorded as the last of his words, is all the more moving against this dark backdrop.

I was once very upset by another poet less cool than Yeats, Dylan Thomas, whose poem to his father turned conventional advice upside down, insisting: "Do not go gentle into that good night." "Rage against the dying of the light," Thomas urged his father. I once presumed to reverse and contradict this message, using the villanelle form in imitation of Thomas. Rebuttal does not now seem so pressing. Let the poem stand in the books, I can now say. Plato, who had his stringent ideas on these subjects long ago, banned the poets from his ideal republic because of the grief and lamentation that their writings stir up; what we need, and our young soldiers particularly need, he taught, is tremendous fortitude and calm in the face of death. Well, the troubling emotions are part of the record. We are not blocks of stone, neither have we quite entered the angelic element.

If at times a mere membrane seems to separate us from the otherworld, as Rilke suggests in his *Duino Elegies*, at others an abyss looms between.

Blessed are those graced with a peaceful ending. They seem to have received a literal answer to the petition "Bring us not to the test," since they have been spared such severe trial. To the degree that we are left on our own, there will be turmoil. Thérèse of Lisieux in her last months was racked with doubts, cast often into desolation. John of the Cross would have his profound explanation of her dark time; secular analysts of our day would have quite another. At the very least we can say that in Thérèse we have someone fully alive, "intense" in all the senses of that word, and by nature resistant to the dark. But she did believe and know and affirm that despite feelings very much to the contrary and in the hold of bewildering moods, she was being carried by God's care. This is what made her a saint.

Dealing with death brings lonely moments, to put it mildly. At the closing time of a life, companionship and support, as we recognize, is essential. But the one in attendance is frequently baffled about what to say. The words have to come from some genuine place, or silence is better. Despite long years as a professional, I find myself more tongue-tied than fluent in such circumstances. It is hard enough when the relationship is calm and settled. But much unfinished business will often lie between us and the people approaching closure. We want to clear things up with them, so as to lessen a hurt they have received or, alas, so as to justify ourselves. We may instinctively look on the final time with someone close to us, short or long, as a last chance to change them – "If only they weren't so you-know-what." But people's minds do not unbend very much in the last stages, do they? Almost everything has to be left to God's mercy then. And there is always the faint possibility that we may not be infallible judges of others.

We continue to have to say good-bye long after the not-quite-loved one, or the twistedly loved one, has gone, and that process will continue – in our thoughts, our writings, our memorial gestures – until the Lord helps us get things right with them. Endings are the hardest part of the creative process. I wonder whether Shakespeare himself did not rush his endings or tire before fully working them out. The pressure on writers in the old days was to provide a happy ending – a distribution of rewards and prizes, as Henry James put it. Dickens, for instance, was pressured by the author Bulwer Lytton to brighten up the ending of *Great Expectations*, which he did, but not to its benefit.

The pressure is opposite today. Nowadays, for us who are mature – so the claim goes – the happy resolution just doesn't play. Yet in this matter, when it comes to our own lives, we do not have the luxury of being morose. To us, a happy ending is vital. We wish, and pray, to achieve our possibilities: to say yes, despite all; to take that step off the end that psychological games now encourage; to turn oneself over to the Lord just as one is, dependent on mercy. I know I am not likely to be in very good shape, in super condition, when the crucial moment comes. My most pressing utterance is likely to be "Help!"

I admire, almost beyond bounds, the young people and others who face death continually for justice' sake. I particularly remember, in San Salvador, a member of the Commission of Human Rights, whom I, along with other U.S. professors, met in 1983. Many of his colleagues had been brutally dealt with. Did he fear? "I go out daily," he told us, "not knowing whether I will come back." Of course he feared. Still we all felt unworthy of such a person.

But each of us going forth from the temporal to the eternal takes an equally bold and uncertain step. Knowing the challenge that each of us faces, dramatic or not, public or individual, and aware that in the last analysis we remain alone, we still look for support wherever available. In the simplest of our daily prayers, also, we turn to Mary, the surest of our intercessors: "Pray for us now and at the hour when we have to deliver."

REFLECTION AND ACTION

Food for Thought:

Spell out your own reaction, past or present, toward the critical, and even terminal, illness of some close friend or family member. The range of possibilities runs from avoidance to gesture of support from a distance, to forcing oneself into an occasional visit, to showing more spontaneous and continued support, to short-or-long-term tending. Such an exercise would aim not at guilt but at awareness.

In regard to yourself, reflect on how you deal with intimations of mortality, especially if you find them dominant.

Suggested Steps:

The last thing we can count on, in our closing days, is a change in our habitual responses. To the extent we are complainers now, we will be so then. Now is the time to start reversing the pattern!

Compose a prayer in which you ask for the sentiments and responses you would like as the time approaches to meet the Lord.

CHAPTER TWO

HUMILITY AND
SELF-UNDERSTANDING

THE GROUNDS FOR PRIDE

No begging. All that parched skin,
its rough grain crunching underfoot,
somehow stores up. The jealous land
sheathes its slim wood, stretches
the pulpy green over pocked wood.
Tiny root systems scour for drink,
or a jab searches deep. Minuscule
desert leaves, water-tight,
uncurl only a brief season.
What thorns! catclaws to
jacket, fishhook in unwary leg.
The toothed visage has its pride.

Skirted trunks await spring
to shoot up a crimson or sun-
yellow flag. Seed abides
the brief time of grass.
An angel-wing-cactus face
this night runs happily with rain.
Ocotillo, cholla, jojoba
out of long patience laugh.
A light fall, steady.

The scrub earth drinks in.

Pronunciation: ocotillo = oh - co - tea - yo
cholla = cho - ya
jojoba = ho - ho - ba

How we bandy about religious language! The people who receive it in dead earnest, if they have no sense of the polyvalence of words, the many shades of negative and positive that words can carry, run considerable danger. This is most true of the terms we use for self-evaluation or to express attitudes taken before others. As a central instance of the above, consider the word "pride." What a discerning spirit we need when we employ it!

We are heirs to medieval and Renaissance literature that bills pride as the worst of the capital sins. In Edmund Spenser's *The Faery Queene,* for instance, the Red Cross knight, in quest of holiness, finds himself decoyed into the House of Pride, an aery and gilded wonder. It is a pasteboard construction, however, and resting on sand. Queen Lucifera sits there disdainfully on her throne, gazing at "her self-loved semblance" in a mirror she holds. The *Spiritual Exercises* of Ignatius Loyola, from that same period, gives us a familiar meditation on Two Standards. "Imagine," says Ignatius, "the enemy of human nature" seated as a chieftain "in that great plain of Babylon, as on a lofty throne of fire and smoke, in aspect horrible and fearful," dispersing demons into the world. The emissaries "are first to tempt people to covet riches (which they are prone to most of the time), so that they may more readily come to the vain honor of the world and thence to unbounded pride."

The scenario arises from the New Testament narrative of the temptations of Christ, from the beatitudes, and from that allusion in the First Letter of John to the triple snare put out by "the world": "the lust of the flesh, and the lust of the eyes, and the pride of life" (Revised Standard Version).

Greek civilization at its height ran the constant risk of this pride of life, *hubris*, the fatal presumption of one convinced of his or her own greatness. Self-vaunting was also a mark of the Renaissance, with its sky-high aspirations and the premium it put on versatility, *sprezzatura*. In the well-known sonnet he addressed to Death, John Donne cast this terror as a strutting courtier. Pointing out how illusory were all Death's victories, the poet asks, "Why swell'st thou then?"

How vividly our authors and spiritual writers have fleshed out the first definition of pride in the *Oxford English Dictionary*: "a high or overweening opinion of one's own qualities, attainments or estate, which gives rise to a feeling or attitude of superiority over others and contempt for them." The Romans called this *superbia* and knew a lot about it. Actors embody *superbia* by a curl of the lip, arch of the eyebrows, upward tilt of the head.

There is not much new under the sun. Temptations repeat themselves, nor do vices change. Nonetheless our day and age seems to suffer less from inordinate self-esteem than from lack of allowable self-esteem – not from the overweening ego but from the starved, unsure, self-absorbed ego. So many people walk off from unfulfilled contracts, take pay for sloppy work, or just leave a mess without remorse – so many seem devoid of self-respect that we find ourselves agreeable to a little resurrecting of the word "pride."

The Oxford English Dictionary helps us with subsequent meanings that give a different valence to "pride": "a consciousness or feeling of what is befitting or due to oneself or one's position, which prevents a person from doing what he considers to be beneath him or unworthy of him." This definition was composed before women asserted some pride via gender-inclusive language! It applies to the well-groomed person, who takes some pride in appearance and alarms friends in a time of sickness or depression by letting himself or herself go. It applies to the old-school workman whom we find downcast after words from a dissatisfied customer. And it applies to the elderly woman hunting through grocery stores and clothing shops for bargains without letting on how tight the pinch is; after all, she has her pride.

A marvelous instance of tranquil self-possession struck me some years ago in poor farm areas of Mexico where young children, often badly fed and clothed and educated, would introduce themselves with a flourish: "Raoul Enrique Morales y Villanueva a sus ordenes," at your orders, or "para servirle," at your service. The same attitude closer to home was voiced by a workman whom psychoanalyst Robert Coles interviewed for his essay "Work and Self-Respect" (in *Adulthood*, ed. E. Erikson): "I have a job and I manage to keep my head above water. If I can do that until my last kid is out of high school and has a job, I'll be able to die with some self-respect."

True enough, our human capacities, even the most exquisite, are not self-originating and have very discernible limits. God blesses us not when we offer thanks for not being like the rest of humanity but when we turn with our frailty and infirmities to ask support. God helps us not be too proud to see a doctor, to admit wrongs, to even ask for support when desperate. Jesus Christ gave us a memorable example, "who though in the form of God did not think being equal to God something to cling to, but poured himself out, taking on the form of a slave."

This "condescension" of Jesus Christ, this stepping down among us, was for the purpose of raising us up, helping us stand erect with him before the Father. "Lift up your heads, O ye gates," says Psalm 24, and Handel has made it an unforgettable chorus for his *Messiah*. Jesus, after "exaltation on the cross," to use that paradoxical term for his debasing death, lifted us up into a new personal identity in which we could rest securely.

The Jesuit poet Gerard Manley Hopkins, as he watched a falcon hovering in a strong wind and mastering it, found in this superb flight ("superb," a fine adjective that the English language has rescued from negative connotation) his most striking image for Christ Our Lord. In "The Windhover" Hopkins cried out in his own Elizabethan version of the praises of the Lamb in the "Apocalypse": "Brute beauty and valor and act, oh, air, pride, plume here / Buckle!" i.e., here fasten together and concentrate. Hopkins struggled with a sense of worthlessness all his life, yet he was a true believing son of Ignatius the hidalgo (*hijo de algo*, son of something big). He founded his sense of worth on the Lord's glory. We find in this line of his poem that positive, or plus, quotient emerging in yet a third *Oxford English Dictionary* definition of pride: "a feeling of elation, pleasure or high satisfaction derived from some action or possession." This is the feeling that comes from being son or daughter of the real Somebody.

REFLECTION AND ACTION

Food for Thought:

Register your own take on the word "pride," what resonance, positive or negative, predominates for you.

Try to sort out in your life what you rightly take pride in, where you are deficient in self-esteem, and where self-importance takes over. This admittedly is a huge order!

Suggested Steps:

Humble gestures, as opposed to humble words, are appropriate in any context where we have pulled rank, brandished authority, strutted and crowed in any way.

In the case of deficient self-esteem, often against strong evidence of one's gifts, changing the perspective may take a lifetime. Continue that change, if begun; begin it, if not. Never let the whispers of low self-worth go without contradiction. *Agere contra*, Ignatius said: Act against them.

HOW AM I DOING?

>   on a responsible body
>   the unhealed spot of itch
>
>   old mail on a desk corner
>   slowdown in absorbing
>
>   in my off-hours room
>   the t.v. watches itself
>
>   you snap at the telephone
>   yet it means no harm
>
>   all I've been looking into
>   changes focal length
>
>   workday like a Chinese painting
>   with its imperfection smudge:
>
>   "how am i doing?"
>   suggest rephrase question

In one of Flannery O'Connor's stories, a beady-eyed girl asks one of the confident adults, "If you're so smart, why ain't you rich?" The conversation stopper. If you have had all the opportunities, the best of education and companionship and challenges, why, midway in the course of life, does the water seem suddenly to have gone out of the bathtub?

That's not how it's supposed to be – not, at least, according to that wisest of adults, Aristotle. In his *Rhetoric*, book 2 (chap. 12-14), treating the arts of persuasion, Aristotle classifies, or types, the various groups who will undergo persuasion – the young, the elderly, those in their prime. He limits his consideration to males, having absorbed the bias, that is to say, the narrowed perception of what it is to be human, that characterized "society" in ancient Greece. Still, his analysis is thought provoking.

Young men, according to Aristotle, are energetic, passionate, not well controlled, inconstant in their desires, hypersensitive, competitive, and generous.

> They trust others readily, because they have not yet often been cheated. . . . They have exalted notions, because they have not yet been humbled by life or learned its necessary limitations. . . . Their lives are regulated more by moral goodness than by calculation. . . . All their mistakes are in the direction of doing things excessively and vehemently. . . . They are shy, accepting the rules of the society in which they have been trained.

The elderly, on the other hand, having made innumerable mistakes, find life on the whole a bad business. They "think" but they never "know," putting a "perhaps" to everything and suspecting evil everywhere. They are temperate, since "they do not feel their passions much." They are self-concerned, tight-fisted (since money is hard to get and harder to keep), utilitarian, and chilled by fears. "They are continually talking about the past, because they enjoy remembering it." Not an attractive picture. Tillie Olsen's story "Tell Me a Riddle" shows us an aging Jewish couple in just those terms, but instead of a caricature proceeds to an account of memorable struggling.

And how about those in their prime? That was the question that drew me to Aristotle in the first place. Ah, they blend control with energy, prudence with generosity, noble aims with practicality. They represent, in short, the perfect mean between extremes. (Yes, one is tempted to say, just ask their wives!) And Aristotle concludes: "The body is in its prime from thirty to thirty-five, the mind about forty-nine." There it is, the model of maturity, the time of ripeness!

Well now, Aristotle, how can your treatment of middle age, which has a certain ring of truth and appears so sensible, especially if one is thirty-seven or thirty-eight, run so counter to life history? Is it not, perhaps, that you view things as a naturalist? This outlook will show you the young creature as vigorous, daring, heavily socialized, needing time, of course, to accumulate experience, and alas, all too soon starting on its downhill course. If you had been older at the time of writing, I doubt you would claim that the old "do not feel their passions much." If you had not been specially nurtured and encouraged in your education, you might have felt much more uncertainty and self-doubt. And if, reflecting on middle age, you had consulted a few women, they would have some tales of diminished esteem, unfair distribution of burdens, deferred objectives, confusion about themselves, to say nothing of infighting within their claustrophobic world, dimming the rosy picture considerably.

To speak of that middle period specifically with its stock of responsibilities, its reliable friends, its proofs of esteem, and its satisfactions – I find myself struck by the side of things that Aristotle glosses over. It comes back to me from one of the old schoolroom poems, "My Lost Youth," of Longfellow.

> I remember the gleams and glooms that dart
> Across the school-boy's brain;
> The song and the silence in the heart,
> That in part are prophecies and in part

Are longings wild and vain.

Longfellow ends each stanza with this refrain: "And the thoughts of youth are long, long thoughts." Precisely. To dream of great enterprises is so much the essence and presupposition of youth, as Erik Erikson has taught, that we draw our very identity from this process, and it points us to all serious accomplishment. The dreams, in that respect, are "prophecies." Without them we are pitiable. But inevitably, too, since their scope is limitless, they prove "wild and vain." What seemed to us most important to achieve so often eludes us. Our children turn out "different," our health falters, opportunity closes off, the world fails to improve, our limitations show themselves, or something even more mysterious happens to temper satisfaction. If only we weren't born with that window on the infinite.

The Fathers of the Church and Fathers of the Desert noticed this discouragement in the monks a long time ago and called it, after Psalm 91, "the noonday devil" or, with Pope Gregory the Great, "the spirit of sadness." Their most common diagnostic term was *acedia*, a kind of sloth bringing the monk to a standstill. It involved a distaste for his community, a hankering for greener pastures, and a sense of making no progress. It appeared to the authorities, from Cassian through Thomas Aquinas, as a form of excessive self-concern, and thus culpable. Seeing and feeling so much of it ourselves, we are slower to judge the culpability, more conscious of middle-aged dissatisfaction as a suffering, an affliction. Paradoxically this condition is grace bearing; it recalls us to our Christian project, giving the form of the Lord's Spirit to our lives precisely at their most problematical. If only our structures did not have to collapse before their reinforcement. I write this from Mexico City a few months after the terrifying earthquake!

We know that without some peaks, life, even the most dedicated life, becomes well-nigh impossible. The times of inspiration and dream are crucial. We all need the moment through which Othello passed when, fresh from his marriage to Desdemona, he exclaimed, "If 'twere now to die, 'twere now to be most happy." But Othello had eventually to come down from this peak, to face his jealousy and gullibility. Virginia Woolf threaded this quotation from Othello through her novel *Mrs. Dalloway*, as a theme. Mrs. Dalloway, high at various moments of human encounter, excited about her forthcoming party, is also fighting off depression, just as her author had continually to do. Her happiness had its bounds.

The theme of happiness being dogged by its contrary even as it seeks its proper focus runs insistently and compellingly through Tolstoy's *Anna Karenina*. Tolstoy's novel follows not just the desperately passionate Anna but also the great landowner and truth-seeker Constantin Levin. Levin reflects much of Tolstoy himself, who was embarking on an anxious religious quest at the very time of adding to this text its final section and giving the whole its last revision.

Early in *Anna Karenina*, Levin, about to propose marriage to the teen-aged Kitty, finds himself near her at an ice rink; a superb skater, he thinks to himself, "This is life! This is happiness!" Fool, she will refuse him in her infatuation with the young, shining officer, Vronsky. But Vronsky sweeps off her brother-in-law's married sister, Anna. The affair quickly becomes a tight, if constricting, bond. The passion changes Vronsky from an adventurer to someone who stakes all (and eventually loses), concentrating on "the only one happiness in life for me – love." Early in their relations, Vronsky arrives one evening to find Anna brooding on the obstacles they face. "You seem unwell or worried. What were you thinking about?"

"Always of the same thing," she said with a smile. She spoke the truth. Whenever, at whatever moment she was asked what she was thinking about, she could have answered unhesitatingly that she was thinking of one thing only – her happiness and her unhappiness. (bk. 2, chap. 22).

Actually, Anna is about to tell Vronsky she is pregnant, but this itself is secondary to her. Unhappiness comes indeed to haunt her – even in her dreams, as a menacing old peasant; and she breaks at the end. When she is about to commit suicide by throwing herself under the train, she is delayed by her handbag; she has to rid herself of it. Taking it off, she thinks to make the gesture that, as a child, she made when entering the water: "She crossed herself." Tolstoy sees Anna, in other words, not just as self-preoccupied and self-tormenting but as one of the Russian sufferers.

Levin is a counterbalance, but also a counterpart, to Anna. Despite his love of farmwork and his absorption with the lot of the peasants, a shadow hovers over him; he is convinced, as are all about him, that all his happiness depends on marriage. Kitty, meanwhile, recovers slowly from her devastating rejection; her brother-in-law then cleverly brings the two together. The marriage ceremony, in spite of Levin's doubts and skepticism (and an awkward sacramental confession helped along by a sensitive old Orthodox priest), is glowing.

And then? Then the new couple have to battle and to talk their way awkwardly through misunderstandings and rifts. Levin's contentment increases, with the birth of a child contributing to it; but so, unaccountably, does his unbelief. Kitty observes the "unhappy state it puts him in," but cannot help. He is driven at times very close to suicide. Then a workman, as they are threshing rye, helps him enormously with his shrewd evaluation of two prosperous peasants known in the country nearby. One, a rich skinflint, "who lives only for himself," prospers. The other's affairs are often precarious because he is lenient with debtors who are in difficulty. The workman comments on the latter, "He lives for his soul, remembers God." That's it, Levin realizes: "To live not for oneself but for God." Pretty basic, one would say. A wonder it took eight hundred pages to get there!

Yet in life as well as art it takes easily that long to catch on. In truth, what matters is our daily service. As living units of the body of the faithful, limbs but also hearts, we have functions sharply defined – confined necessarily, yet essential to the whole. We belong and we matter. Our satisfaction, the secret of our existence, comes from living as we are called to live before God at a given time, with what love we can, despite the confusion. This, more than doing well in our own eyes, fulfills our human calling, our recurrent good dream. Naturally, we say to ourselves daily, "OK, I know that's true, but if only . . ." But we can also answer ourselves: "Oh, please, shut up!"

And this is just the beginning of an answer. The whole of it has to emerge from within the paschal mystery, our identification with Christ in his sufferings, and his deep-rooted happiness. This was the extra dimension or even corrective that Dostoevski, in his tormented but profound stories, brought consciously to his great contemporary Tolstoy. In *Crime and Punishment*, for instance, we find suffering almost a value in itself, an excruciating presence before which the others in moments of insight have to bow. Raskolnikov, the young student deluded by a kind of Napoleonic pride, is reminded by the police inspector Porfiry what tremendous force the belief has, among many Russian peasants, that "one must suffer."

We instinctively recoil here. The contemporary mind, daily apprised of new injustices, rejects nothing more indignantly than unnecessary suffering. And yet each life has a necessary suffering inscribed within it, through which our birth takes place. The process of continual conversion means, above all, accepting that. As Raskolnikov struggles with the decision whether or not to confess to the double murder he committed, Sonia, the prostitute, offers him a small cross, which her stepmother in her misery had worn. When finally resolved to own up, he accepts it. In the epilogue, when Raskolnikov in Siberia is expiating what he still will not admit to be a crime, sullen and self-absorbed, he finds himself impelled to bow, to break open, one day before Sonia, who has kept stubbornly loyal. Happiness, a new experience for both, comes upon them. The author notes, however, in concluding: "Raskolnikov did not then know that the new life would not be given them for nothing, . . . that it would cost him great striving, great suffering. But that is the beginning of a new story." Yes, at least eight hundred pages more!

REFLECTION AND ACTION

Food for Thought:
Recount your principal dream or dreams in youth, then delineate how the present seems by comparison. Emphasize the positive role dreams have played, but be truthful about frustrations or tempering, in other words about what these dreams may have suffered.

Reflect on happiness in your life, that is, on what should make you happy and what actually does or doesn't.

Suggested Steps:
This chapter speaks of "middle-aged dissatisfaction" as recalling us "to our Christian project." In prayer, converse with Our Lord, or with his holy mother, or with your patron saint about how, in view of any tempering of dreams, you can be true to this project.

THE HEART'S FLING

"The One Room"

I am with you in the one room
too late for thinking ourselves outside
each other's smell familiar

In and out of each other's arms
the distance varying
some scratches won't scab over

At odd moments, you know, love
as with your quizzical look
I mean who could understand why?

Our hands hardly keep to themselves
turning things over and over
impress of flesh from bone

What did you just say? you would
I know the jokes, silences, and high signs
you are pure mystery

Some days I'm difficult?
One who adds plus to minus
has enclosed us here

The terminology of Christian life used to abound in phrases like "self-sacrifice," to say nothing of "self-denial," concepts that one is now apologetic about raising. Gone, like the Lenten fast.

Root out self-will, we used to be told. Ignatius of Loyola insisted with his followers that holiness lies in mortification, the readiness to leave off what you are stubbornly and determinedly bent on doing or what you are bending someone else to allow you to do. Certain preachers and spiritual writers gave this notion of mortification a bronco-busting slant and contributed unwittingly to its decline.

Do not be self-centered, we were told as children. That was before Piaget and other students of child development reminded us there is a quite normal egocentric stage. And Freud has made ego respectable beyond almost anything else in his system. Not that Piaget and Freud are gospel; if we have learned anything, it is that psychology does not supplant religious wisdom. But the ground is now less sure, and we are called to correct some crude ways of conceiving things.

The corrections themselves may be just as crude. Message bearers now emphasize the care and feeding of the self as of some exotic plant. "Pamper yourself. Do you secretly desire something? Do it! Be it!" This is the spirit of the times. Is it a huge self-indulgence or does it contain some seed of the true, some response to an unsatisfied need?

Huge numbers of people today suffer from a diminished sense of self. The mega-world pressing in on them seems to squeeze out the sense of being a valuable person. They are undeclared in college, undecided in their political party and religion, with a square of themselves uncommitted in human relations. The ideal of Saint Joseph, *amans nesciri*, happy to be unknown, strikes terror, the menace of nonbeing, into those still searching for identity. Other saints make us uneasy too, like Catherine of Siena in the fourteenth century praying to Christ to take away the last traces of her own will. Yet she did not lack for ego strength, not her, the woman who wrote to a vacillating pope, "Be a man!"

So many factors today attenuate our sense of being real: long years of study, the worm of self-consciousness, confusions of conscience, the sense of being anonymous in a crowd, our helplessness in the face of weapons. How to be somebody? What somebody to be? We fear declaring the death of the self before it has come to life, or directing hatred against the self before we have come to love. What are we to make of the paradoxical language that Jesus keeps addressing to us? We are driven back to it continually as to a nucleus of spiritual health and the distinctive note of the call of discipleship, a summary of the world's religious wisdom.

> Whoever wishes to come after me must deny the self, take up the cross, and follow me. The one anxious to preserve life will lose it; the one who gives up life for me will find it. What does it profit someone to gain all the world but lose one's soul? What exchange can one make for the soul? (Matthew 16:24-27)

These words, this message, we are told, came powerfully from the lips of Dorothy Day, whose attachment to the Lord was never in question. Those who are parents or teachers, graduating their young into the roiled forum of the world, still shudder at the possibility of those dear to them selling their soul, quietly letting go an ideal, compromising to get ahead, not marrying for love, taking a bribe, neglecting a major talent, closing their eyes to some shame.

The call to discipleship issued by Jesus to the young rich man found his generosity wanting. The disciples and Jesus too admitted the human impossibility of taking up this call. Dietrich Bonhoeffer, knowing the terrible burden imposed by life in Nazi Germany to be far beyond the inherent powers of any young man or woman to shoulder, no matter how richly endowed, had a glimmering of true selflessness.

> To deny oneself is to be aware only of Christ and no more of self, to see only him who goes before and no more the road which is too hard for us. Once more, all that self-denial can say is, "He leads the way, keep close to Him." (*The Call to Discipleship*)

So the secret is a great love, a fling of the heart. St. Augustine was voicing not so much a stern ascetic command as a

utopian dream when he pictured the city of God being built
by the love of God growing into the contempt of self. "Contempt of self" and "contempt of the world" are troubling
phrases that tend to go sour unless sweetened with the
awareness of love (God's, who "so loved the world") and of
lovableness (ours, because Jesus Christ "loved me and de-
livered himself for me").

The Song of Songs celebrates the impulse to self-forgetfulness in intense young love. Its literal subject, one we
are not meant to bypass, is love between the sexes, genuine
romance. But in the theistic view, "love is of God" and tutors
us in God. Hence Jews and Christians have mostly read the
Song of Songs as a metaphor for God drawing his people
tenderly and passionately and eliciting the response of the
soul, i.e., of the whole person from deep inside. This combination of the ardent and the arduous, of the supremely
sensitive and the self-forgetful, is exquisitely caught in the
poems of Saint John of the Cross.

Sexual love, or romance, what couples would like to
think is "love stronger than death," can be quite ambivalent,
can have a lot of selfishness to it. Yet it affords us our prime
experience of self-forgetfulness. The lover is by no means
unaware of pleasure, exaltation, and a sense of well-being.
But the other person is the focus. The lover is ready to go
to any lengths, sacrifice all comforts and even future hopes,
just as St. Paul did when he cried out his love for his fellow
Jews: "I could wish that I myself were accursed and cut off
from Christ for the sake of my brethren, my kinsmen by
race."

In a remarkable prayer-poem the Chilean poet Gabriela
Mistral pleads for her young lover, who, much troubled, had
committed suicide in the course of their romance. She goes
beyond the grave to argue on his behalf with God (the
translation is by Langston Hughes).

You say he was cruel? You forget I loved him ever.
He knew my wounded flesh was his to shatter.
Now the waters of my gladness he disturbs forever?
I loved him! You know I loved him – so that does not
  matter.
To love (as You well understand) is a bitter task.

A Japanese novelette, *The Hunting Gun,* by Yasushi Inoue,
recounts the following episode. In a girl's school, the students are studying the active and passive voices of English
verbs. A girl passes a paper around asking, "Which do you
prefer, 'to love' or 'to be loved'?" All, including Saito, the
story's central figure, check "to be loved," except for the
last person, a "gloomy girl," who boldly circles the opposite.
What Saito comes to realize later, at the end of her fling,
her long adulterous affair, is that despite its exalting moments and her great burden of happiness (as Inoue puts
it), she has failed her true husband and has missed her
calling to love.

More and more these days I meet women and men who
were once in religious orders, or holy orders, and in whom
still, whether married or single, the pull of the ideal, the
spirit of devotion, and even a certain unworldliness are quite
evident. One does not conclude that their spirit of self-sacrifice has faltered. Could it be that they failed to find in
religious life or parish rectories the environment for a great
love?

T. S. Eliot had some idea of this consuming love when
he devised his fleeting image of "Christ the tiger" ("Geron-
tion"). He embodied it later in the figure of Celia Co-
plestone of *The Cocktail Party,* choosing the dangerous service
of the gospel as a greater context for her love than that of
an unsatisfactory affair. We keep remembering the four
American women who were murdered in El Salvador in
1980, with awe and gratitude for the great love they enacted.

To conclude: What we live by and are galvanized by is still the type of action that awed Gerard Manley Hopkins and drew him to compose his long poem "The Wreck of the Deutschland." On a ship full of distraught passengers foundering in a storm off the English coast a Franciscan nun was heard crying out above the storm in welcome to Christ. The hidden gift of this poem is in recording the writer's own response to this nun's heroism, how in a visit to the chapel he found his own devotion enkindled by it. As he tells it, he "fled with a fling of the heart to the heart of the Host." Everything that can help us live in this way is precious.

REFLECTION AND ACTION

Food for Thought:

Does the ideal of self-effacement, *amans nesciri*, appeal to you or, by contrast, carry some threat? In your own case, try to visualize, or to indicate, how you see your "self" before God – as partly undiscovered perhaps, as wounded and recuperating (or not recuperating yet), as uneasy, as having a discernible and mostly positive shape, maybe even (which is to be hoped) as peaceful and assured. "Several of the above" may be the sensible answer.

Assess how dependent you are on the good opinion of others and, slightly narrower, how anxious you are to make a good impression.

Suggested Steps:

Do a few random acts of kindness, perhaps even anonymous ones, so as to exercise the option "to love."

The above may apply also to religious devotion – something beyond the planned or the expected.

THE SHOUTING HOUSE

Baby Joe squalling
Mama yelling downstairs
Benny shooing the cat off his bed
Mary Kate in her room with the Rolling Stones
    full blast
Murphy wisecracking out his window to a girlfriend
Aunt Bertha scolding about the bathroom
Papa coming home, standing in the front door,
Hollering, "What's all the awful noise?"
Everybody shouting in the shouting house.

Saturday, volume up high.
Bicycles get the dog in a stew
Aunt Bertha bawls out delivery boys
The strap is at work on Benny
Papa's irate: "Murphy, where did you put those keys?"
Baby Joe throws toys all over his room
Mama has Mary Kate locked in and arguing
Outcries, a crash, doors slamming, feet on the run
Every sound of shouting from the shouting house.

Sunday, the blessed pause.
T.V. is off
The hound has curled up in the yard
Benny puts on his good behavior
Baby Joe beams from his sister's arms
Aunt Bertha swallows her growls
Mama wears her face smooth as a pond
Murphy stands with his arm hooked in his mother's
Papa gets the car purring in the garage
Away they go
Reprieve
Not a breath of shouting from the shouting house.

I lived next door to the shouting house for a year and a half in Tuskegee, Alabama, and met its family members weekly at church. It exercised a kind of horrible fascination upon me, as well as tickling my funny bone. My own younger days were mostly without household turbulence, except for times when I infringed on my younger brother and he defended himself. Nothing all-out and consistent. So the place next door seemed human (quite human, in fact) in a way I was unfamiliar with. Since then a fair number of people have told me, upon hearing the poem read, "Yes, we lived next to the same house," or "That's our house you were writing about."

Why my renewed fascination with this episode of a dozen years ago? Because we have come upon days, alas, when the central subject is aggressivity and the ways of defusing, or socializing, or harnessing it. Right handling of aggressivity is a matter of life or death, not just for individuals walking the city streets but for the human family as a whole.

Erich Fromm holds to a distinction between aggressivity and what he calls self-assertion; the latter, which he says has nothing to do with wounding people, is proper, for example, to the male in his sexual role and in fact to anyone "moving forward toward a goal without undue hesitation, doubt, or fear" (*The Anatomy of Human Destructiveness* [New York: Holt, Rinehart and Winston, 1973]). This distinction between the bruiser, one who relishes attacking, and the normal feisty person is quite appropriate and necessary. Still, Fromm seems to presuppose a pre-Newtonian state of things, where no galling is caused by bodies moving forward to a legitimate goal. Both biology and psychology are more likely to speak of self-assertion and aggressivity as closely, if uneasily, bound. Even the normal dynamics seem to have some measure of suffering built in.

Konrad Lorenz has maintained that the aggressive instinct is inseparable from our animal origins and is vital in some way to everyone, even within the most intimate human bonds. To contain and integrate the aggressive drive within a bond of friendship is, as he points out in *On Aggression,* quite difficult in today's overcrowded and acquisitive conditions. Yet the unleashing of it, anarchy leading to a kind of social meltdown, is an alternative all too familiar in our century and not to be entertained for a minute. Lorenz, speaking unfavorably of most contemporary forms of competition, does make an exception for sports, with its strict rules, its elicitation of heroics, its arbiters (they above all), and the many cross-team friendships. Yet sports too, by unleashing a militant enthusiasm, can cater to the worst in us.

Lorenz affirmed that reason and moral responsibility first came into the world with humans, to keep wildness in control. But he speaks more convincingly when demonstrating the intelligence already at work in nature, where definite restraints keep animals of the same species from abusing one another with their own weaponry. Energy and control, impulse and direction were meant to be coordinates from the start of animal life. We have warped the collaboration in many ways, ready as we are to fabricate images of enemies to hate. What a paradox we present, Lorenz exclaims.

> The only being capable of dedicating himself to the very highest moral and ethical values requires for this purpose a phylogenetically adapted mechanism of behavior whose animal properties bring with them the danger that he will kill his brother, convinced that he is doing so in the interests of these very same high values. Ecce homo! (p. 274)

Rollo May contributed to our understanding of explosive human energies with his category of the *daimon,* as explained in two central chapters of *Love and Will.* Though the concept of *daimon,* stressing as it does our natural tie with the divine, seems to point in an opposite direction from

Lorenz, upward rather than backward to animal origins, it gives us a great deal of insight into aggressiveness. For the *daimon* is, by definition, a generative impulse, the urge "in every being to affirm itself, assert itself, perpetuate and increase itself" (p. 123). The assertion can be blind and devastating; Dante's *Inferno* teems with images of the daimonic gone awry. On the other hand, it can also carry us to "impossible" heights of creativity, public achievement, and the passionate attachment that is "strong as death" (*Song of Songs* 8, 6).

In May's sobering evaluation, our aggressive side, the daimonic, tends to defy control, burst limits, have us at its mercy. What a blow to our narcissism it is, says he. Yet it does not cancel our free will, and we are pathetic without it. Repression is convenient to religions, classrooms, domestic settings, industrial life, civil society. "But we cannot avoid the toll of apathy and the tendency toward later explosion which such repression brings in its wake" (p. 123).

The repressed stage is well described by Joyce Carol Oates in a vignette from one of her stories: "She was sweet and apologetic, as always, as she had been all her life, nervously backing away from the arguments she should have had with my father, turning aside from the talks she should have had with me." One of the troubling insights of modern psychology is that often, in a person such as the one described above, aggression goes underground. The ignoble and hurtful form it assumes is called passive aggression, where people taking a silent and apparently meek stance are in reality resistant, manipulative, and revengeful. It has wreaked havoc in religious life, to say nothing of marriages. Far better the ability to slug it out.

As I think of people slugging it out, I wonder now, years later, what has become of the members of the shouting house, how they have bestowed their loves, what callings they have followed and how effectively, what insights they have come to about themselves, how well they can now compose differences, how happily they move among people. I hope that they do not lose heart as they look out with adult awareness upon the naked force that has been rampant in the world since the days of the *Iliad* (see Simone Weil's astonishing essay "The Iliad, or The Poem of Force"). I hope above all that the gospel, framing its call to love often in terms of confrontation, endurance, and strong resolve, still today and now more than ever gives them heart.

REFLECTION AND ACTION

Food for Thought:
Locate yourself on the spectrum of self-assertion, which can verge into aggressivity or invert into passive aggression. Describe yourself, in other words, in terms of this chapter.

A parallel but related spectrum is that of sensitivity, where the male defect tends to be insensitivity and the female, hypersensitivity, yet the individual defies the generality.

Suggested Steps:
Practical steps would need to follow from the self-description above. Identify areas where you exceed or fall short, where you are like a bull in a china shop or like an open wound, and decide on countermeasures.

CHAPTER THREE

AFFECTION, FRIENDSHIP, COMMUNITY

CICERO TO ATTICUS: HI!

So who was sitting at the table there
in the place now empty
someone inquires, coming with a full plate,
and we can't remember

We recall an argument full of repartee
and of the revolving presences
wasn't the one we are reaching for
heatedly at the center?

It comes back. Someone, to tweak the master,
put Cicero on the scales against Virgil,
claiming the moralist to weigh more
than the unspeakable sorrow of Troy.

How he bridled at such inanity,
the owner of that surprising bass.
How the old master's cheeks glowed
and his eyes, touching on a loved author.

Well, he was our lesson *de amicitia*
who dropped any paperwork in hand
at a knock when we came nosing to Paris,
and he never threw away a letter.

Not unfamiliar with the woes,
he flamed wickedly at our critics
and crowed at our small victories.
He could fuss and sniff. So?

How his approving eyes store up
seat by seat at a family dinner.
At the sacred table he led quietly,
intently, and that's where we'll find him.

SANTIAGO, CHILE: WINTER 1989

It is refreshing, along the crowded sidewalks of the Avenida
O'Higgins, to see young girls, three or four abreast, with
their arms about each other's waist, and slightly older boys
shoulder to shoulder. There are kissing couples enough in
the Metro and along the quieter streets; the fast friendships
of the very young hold my attention for now. Our latter days
seem to throw us back to our earliest. As one gets older,
friendship gets very precious again. Perhaps it is the loss of
someone close, or the breaking of a circle, that makes us
more aware of the value of friendship at a certain age.

In saying the above, perhaps what I do is generalize
from my own experience, having spared less time for friends
at a busier or more anxious stage. Anyway, for the purpose
of later-life illumination, a scene comes back to me now
from my youth. My mother and brother and I, with cousins
and aunts, used to spend summers in a rambling Italian-style
country place with an orchard and a vegetable garden and

beds of marigold and zinnia. The men were at work in "The City." Every evening that I can remember, our caretaker Giulio retired to his porch behind his screen door with his friend Mattaioli. They talked some, very low, but mostly they smoked their pipes. Giulio's wife, Eda, and his son Ernie, our playmate, occupied themselves somehow behind the scenes. That's how it was for years.

Few of us experience friendship as a silent, long smoking of pipes. It is probably most often a phone call: "You are not going to believe this." "Hi, are you feeling any better?" "I've got to get something out of my system." "Listen, I've got a problem." "Hey, guess what – they gave me the job." "What a bummer, they picked someone else." "You heard what so-and-so is preaching? I'd like your frank opinion." "Hello, just touching base." "Are you free for lunch?"

Friends truly give life its salt. They tend, more often than not, to be of the same sex because of natural affinities. Ease seems to be a special mark of friendship. Across the gender line there is a charge in the air that can complicate the easiness, although often enhancing it. Over time and as people grow, *la différence* fades. A good heart, a wise head, a shared depth across any difference of gender, age, or culture truly draw people to one another. The great friendships of the world go in all directions: Huck Finn and Jim, Harold and Maude, St. Benedict and his sister St. Scholastica, Thomas More and the prickly Erasmus, Catherine of Siena and her disciple Fra Tommaso, Sor Juana de la Cruz and the wife of the viceroy of Mexico, Edith Wharton and Henry James.

The vocation of married couples, it would seem, is to become the fastest of friends and, indeed, the most relaxed of friends. "Elementary," as Holmes would say to Watson – but by no means automatic. So much tempering and mellowing and sharing of faith needs to happen; exhaustion, anxiety, personality weakness can so readily block it. Do many of the marriages that fail today go sour because couples fail to achieve friendship, a much more explicit goal than it once was? Maybe the Church will get around to canonizing couples. We might begin with Jacques and Raissa Maritain. Christian social action in the midcentury, not just in Europe but worldwide, took its encouragement and impetus from Jacques; he in turn drew a large measure of conviction and inspiration from his wife.

When it comes to friendship, my mind swings back instinctively to something encountered in my earliest days of Latin studies, the formula opening some letters by the world's most famous orator: *Cicero Attico sal.* Although it means "salt," *sal* is used here as a short form of *salus*, or health. In fact, the complete formula is *salutem plurimam dicit*: "Cicero to Atticus wishes him the best of health." There was a flow of such letters – small talk, news, some unburdening – letters being, after all, a prime channel of friendship. And to Atticus, Cicero dedicated his treatise *De Amicitia* (*On Friendship*) for generations of young scholars to labor through and maybe, years later, to appreciate for its relevance to their lives. In this essay Cicero imagines that Laelius, an upstanding Roman, is reminiscing about his close friend Scipio Africanus the Younger. Laelius tells what he has learned about friendship from Scipio.

> I judge myself to have lived happily because it was side by side with Scipio. . . . We reached the fullest accord in our decisions, our interests, our opinions, which is the real strength of friendship. . . . What is more pleasing than to have someone to whom you can express things as openly as to yourself? What savor would success have, if there were not someone to be as happy about it as yourself? Wouldn't it be harder to bear the blows without someone who feels them more keenly than you do?"
> (*On Friendship*, sec. 4, 6)

Cicero's moralizing tended to the abstract, but in the above essay it drew its life, its savor, from the bond between

Laelius and Scipio. I started this essay and the accompanying poem in an abstract vein, provoked by a question someone asked me about a well-known priest in our community who had just died: "Do you miss him?" I had to be honest with myself that I didn't quite. In consequence, I had to explore the sort of rotating communities we have, where a gap is opened up and someone moves in to fill it. Meanwhile another Jesuit died whom quite a few of us really do miss because he concentrated on friendship. He was Maurice Belval, S.J., longtime student in Paris and companion to those visiting Paris, as well as teacher of Latin and Gregorian music and French. The poem came out of its amorphous state when he entered it.

I now find myself in Chile, where those in contact with Communist Party members report an unsettling impression. These are single-minded people. They are distinctive for their discipline, their austerity, their group-and-class commitment. They have very cool heads. (There was chaos in the Allende socialist regime of 1970 to 1973, but not of Communist making.) But this coolness has a chilling side. It can translate into a dismissiveness in individuals, into zero warmth on contact. Among such intense partisans, the New Testament message of the two commandments, the two directions of love, comes as something new when it is recognizably and compellingly embodied.

I note something of a parallel. Austerity, a watch over the heart, a commitment to the directives and missions of the order – that is how I learned the religious vows, which I am hardly about to repudiate. Did our skin tend often to harden? There are some indications it did. In any case, I find that the sense of companionship, or society, intimated in my way of life, even in the initials I add to my name, does not go without saying – has to be activated, become a spirit, a life-giving dimension. Each of us has to have at our center a heart. Elementary! Our own poor hearts, we find early, are quite insufficient. But befriended beyond the expectations of our poverty, followers of the one unfailing Friend, included surprisingly in the one comprehensive body, we can go forth befriending, inclusive, faithful – in sum, as true hearts.

REFLECTION AND ACTION

Food for Thought:

Some people have a few very close friends, others a much wider range; some have fewer than they would like; some tend to keep to themselves. Measure how much of the salt of friendship you have in your life.

What a commitment friendship is, not excluding the debt of honesty. Do you find that you make a good friend?

Suggested Steps:

African-American poet Langston Hughes, wrote: "Ever' friend you find seems / like they try to do you bad" ("Bound No'th Blues"). I hope this has not been your experience. If so, besides self-protectiveness, some more generous or hopeful pattern of response to others seems in order. Time to initiate it. Determine what you still owe to friendship – attentiveness, patience, the effort of letter writing or calls, honesty, even intervention – and then begin.

THE FAMILY ALBUM

"DUST"

> Dust, how you do fly up
> veil lifts at a touch
> from the floppy album
>> Olga, Bea, in white
>> dresses and broad hats

hair clipped and black,
Carlo under his boater
eyes shaded, the chaperone

each locus cleanly identified –
Mentone, Venice – in white ink
Whose hand?

The Family. in deck chairs
leaning close, upon running boards
sprawling in composition

Dust, you are man,
woman, clustering
no two alike
alloys of mischief
and a high intent

like Uncle Charlie's five
composed a moment in short
pants or the girl tots
my father's hefting
in the wheelbarrow where
you can just see Jackie's
white snout

If you withdraw, spirit
we return to dust.
Never. Shot through with burning.
Remember, dust.

For years a scene has stayed with me from Katherine Ann
Porter's great family story "Old Mortality." Miranda, a young
woman who has recently eloped, is traveling back by train
to her family's hometown for her Uncle Gabriel's funeral.

With her is Cousin Eva. Poor Cousin Eva, utterly homely, has been the butt of family jokes for years. In her long monologue to Miranda, she lets all her bitterness gather and come out. When they had made fun of her, they were all so amusing, she recollects.

> "No harm meant – oh, no, no harm at all. That is the hellish thing about it. It is that I can't forgive," she cried out, and she twisted her hands together as if they were rags. "Ah, the family," she said, releasing her breath and sitting back quietly, "the whole hideous institution should be wiped from the face of the earth. It is the root of all human wrongs," she ended, and relaxed, and her face became calm.

Cousin Eva's indictment seems final and definitive. But when the two of them descend at the station platform to be met by Miranda's father, it is Eva who falls right in with him, pleasantly and affectionately, as if forgetting what she had just said, and he, ignoring his errant daughter, greets her warmly.

"Ah the family!" Who has not thought that? It sometimes seems the epitome of the mixed blessing. Hostilities small or large, bewilderment for years, a sort of inarticulate resentment coexist with genuine affection, forgivable pride, deep satisfaction. The novelist has a way of celebrating this complexity, often with a wry smile, as we have just seen. Some writers, like Thomas Wolfe, can never get far enough outside the network of their own experience to be at ease with it and to get it fully into perspective. Others, like James Agee in *A Death in the Family*, more accurately chronicle the tensions and sorrows, the tenderness and courage, of their own people. Most of us, in what we think or say about the family, draw closer to the professional storyteller than to the battery of experts who generalize about it in print. We engage in oral history, which we often color in the interests of nostalgia or waspish humor.

There is still a strong tendency to make a cult of The Family. In a world that to its aging members seems ever more ruthless, nonreligious, and pornographic, no wonder that some quarters react with a loud call back to "family values." What might these family values be? Loyalty among family members, common interests, mutual concern, ease and affection, readiness to help out in emergencies – all these should be on the list. To the young, "family" also implies a certain discipline; and to all, a code of religious practice, which is a piety and an ethic in one.

Family is a formidable reality. Males, when they hear a feminist lament that women are kept so powerless, think to themselves about the formative power of their mothers and mutter, "Give me a break." Women, for their part, remember growing up under a double standard or marrying into a quasicorporation and mutter back, "Give *me* a break." There are many caricatures, or distortions, of family loyalty (just as there are many possible versions of *The Godfather*); there are stifling family pieties and harsh disciplines; and the whole notion of family property carries an electric charge – so "family" can be a loaded as well as a richly suggestive term.

Suddenly we are back to Cousin Eva and her outburst, and to Miranda and her ostracism, both of which derived from Katherine Ann Porter's marital history, her fierce independence, and her rankling anger. Sigmund Freud was able to give credit to the novelists for preceding, with their remarkable insight, the formulations of psychology (see Lionel Trilling, "Freud and Literature," in *Critical Theory Since Plato*, ed. Hazard Adams). The decades since "Old Mortality" have seen a flood of treatises on the family, training a glaring light on all that is problematic and oppressive. Probably none of these is more scathing than *The Death of the Family*, by the English psychiatrist David Cooper, appearing in the early 1970s. Cooper indicted the family structure for the way it forces people, supposedly, to define themselves as mirror images of others. In setting forth roles and personality models with unmistakable sharpness, the family, he thought, does not leave the individual any room to be such.

Cooper's outcry of distaste, culminating in a "Last Will and Testament" where absolutely nothing was to be left to the family, proceeded from clinical experience of the sufferings of people whose parents or families never gave them a chance. It also, however, had Sartrean, or existentialistic, implications, i.e., that we are to be the formers and creators of ourselves. This is a very unsocial view of reality. Biologically, sociologically, and religiously it is inconceivable that we not be formed in a family. The family is an environment of people conveying to us the habits and attitudes, and eliciting the affections and attachments, that are crucial to being human.

The human being, in the process of growth, is called to mature within some sort of family confines. Maturing is a process of becoming an individual, taking responsibility for ourselves before God – but not in isolation from others. The challenge, actually, is to become somebody within a circle of humans, taking stock of ourselves vis a vis others, forming and asserting convictions in the process of hot debate, often daring things that the protective scheme does not easily allow for. As we think back on our families, we need to be frank, not nostalgic, not ready to gloss over the shortcomings – some grave, some even crippling. But we find ourselves impelled also to recognize and celebrate those genuine marks of attention, all the fostering of our gifts, that took place there. In some cases the neglect or mistreatment will have been, perhaps, criminal; but that is not the rule. It takes only an hour or two in the company of a young family to be reminded how much nurturing, what exhausting attention, a young human being requires moment by moment. To take all of that for granted, to write it off, would seem the epitome of thanklessness.

Humor, no doubt, is essential to dealing with the experience of family. Katherine Ann Porter had it. Family lore is full of it. Sex, romance, slowness in learning, blockages in growing up, misunderstandings – all have their funny side. Bill Cosby has built on that. "Smile, this is going to hurt," he often seems to say. Dolores Curran, writing and lecturing widely among U.S. Catholics, conveys a very positive image of family life by her wit, which she applies to wide domestic experience. Perhaps we chuckle at the aphorism "Family are people you wouldn't choose for friends." We do so, not, please God, for lack of friends among our relatives. It is because difficult people have a way of sticking in the ones around them like splinters. But these provocative people, the ones you have trouble dealing with, carry their own special value. They clarify issues for you, they try your patience, they can even bring home some unwelcome truth.

The concept of religious institutes as families has been around for a long time. Those with some experience of religious life can attest to stifling situations, to the suffering caused by "in-groups," and to survival by humor as well. Ignatius of Loyola is still felt by many to be a stern patriarchal force; this image of him, where it persists, will not quickly yield to argument. Ignatius did certainly insist on detachment from the family – the family of status and means. In a world run by the noble families, exerting their very strong pull, there was ample reason, originally, to limit one's contact. An appreciation of freedom of choice and mature decision was high among the qualities of Ignatius. If religious families, over the centuries, took on some of that shadow aspect of the controlling family, this was and is a condition calling for remedy. But an idyllic final condition is hardly to be expected, for tensions between the individual and the group are bound to continue as long as either is viable, and the tensions can indeed be fruitful.

Family history on any level deserves to be well recorded; but it often takes some distancing – say into one's forties – before we can deal calmly enough with it. My earliest oral history notes begin in the early 1970s. Rereading them now I find my mother recalling that when she and her sisters were in high school (circa 1910), their mother used to read the letters they received. Often my mother was embarrassed to show the letters, she said, because of poor phrasing and spelling. Here am I now, in 1988, with years and years as a college English teacher, still chafing at the same thing among my students, and convinced that I have before me evidence of a New Dark Age! My mother also recalled that her mother did not want her older sister, my aunt Aimee, to enter the Religious of the Sacred Heart because their visiting rules were so strict, even in time of death, and because they oversheltered their members. This set up a tension within my aunt, a very determined person but one upon whom family values had been exerted strongly. Not until her mother's death four years later did she feel free to enter.

Call the family an "institution," if you will; the truer picture is that of a live organism, and of throbbing people. Robert Frost, one expressive citizen of our century, had an excruciating experience of family, both as child and as parent. This is not reflected overtly in his poetry, which does not deal openly with facts of his life. Nonetheless his effort to get the right perspective gave us his touching poem "The Death of the Hired Man." Silas, a wandering odd-jobs man, ignored over the years by his better-off brother, comes in his final days to seek refuge with a fruit grower who has employed him. "He has come home to die," the grower's wife says. The husband comments sardonically, "Home is the place, where, when you have to go there, / they have to take you in." The wife corrects him: "I should have called it / something you somehow haven't to deserve."

Home, the true family place, in other words, is somewhere we belong. Numberless adults, it is undeniable, are conscious only of having been abused, abandoned, or unloved by those whose responsibility it was to nurture them. Homeless, familyless, in an affective way, they look and in fact yearn for better. Scarred as they are, can they hope to find it? Perhaps we need to say, above all, that the more experience one has of distortions, anguish, and ruptures within the family circle, the more effectively one is reminded that in the last analysis, only the "blessed community" is true family.

This reality, the "blessed community," or "communion of saints," by which, according to Thomas R. Kelley, "we overleap the boundaries of church membership [toward other] lives immersed and drowned in God" (*A Testament of Devotion*), is by definition elusive, an object of faith. We live nonetheless for those moments when, as Kelley says, "with a 'chance' conversation we know that we have found and been found by another member of the Blessed Community." We connect with such people, perhaps even in a stable way. This becomes the underlying family of our lives, one to which "the incident of death puts no boundaries."

We are family formers on a large scale, as an essential of our Christian vocation. Still, an important fact remains about this deepest of human callings: it is connected humbly to that inescapable and primal human project, the nuclear family. We take our origin and root, we derive our sense of the desirable society, from the flesh-and-blood family that, with a huge investment of energy and care, gives us our start. We draw our particularity there, and exercise it first of all there, and owe much love and attention to those who are there, even as we move to a wider communion, a more comprehensive human circle, the one in which God's love fully comprehends, grasps, or embraces us.

REFLECTION AND ACTION

Food for Thought:

Be frank, and not nostalgic, nor bitter either (as well as you can manage that) about your experience of family. Try to determine its highlights and pluses, above all, but without omitting the shadows and limitations.

Identify the kind of resonance exerted on you by the word "home," indicating the locales that you think of in this regard.

There is much palaver, let us call it, much rhetoric about "community." Try to gauge to what degree your actual experience of community approaches, or remains distant from, the ideal proposed by Thomas Kelley of the "blessed community."

Suggested Steps:

Exert yourself in activities that foster the "blessed community." These could be liturgical and parochial, they could be geared to implementing the social gospel, they could aim at reconciliation and strengthening of a specific family or quasi-family.

ACCOMPANIMENT

Mom, Pop, Tante Nori, Uncle Vince
loll in the Russian River.
Smiles go round and who knows
what chatter. The frames jitter.
Can't believe I'm now older than they.

Aunt and Uncle take off at a run
after their girls in bonnets,

sunsuits, squealing with terror.
It's for the camera. A grandson
splices this romp together.

The lurid myths of a murder attempt
on parents and our pricy
Freudian sleuths miss something.
Motive wanes. We keep
finding their hands in ours.

Seriously. That trickster Time
eggs us to scenarios of blood
that as eyes open we laugh at,
meeting up in the Great Woods
to decipher the leads home.

A young-adult relative has long intrigued me by addressing
her mother, my cousin Yvonne, a woman of some dignity,
simply as "Vonnie." A Jesuit friend used to speak of his
mother, when she was alive (and quite alive!), by her given
name, Frieda. I remember too three young men born in
England who always referred to their mother by her first
name, Lovene. How strange I used to think. It sounds like
they're objectifying, distancing their own flesh and blood.
And how presumptuous (that was my real problem) this
referring to one's parent as, well, an equal.

I could never have imagined calling my mother "Bea-
trice" – though my favorite author, Dante, filled the name
with a warmth of meaning. Undue familiarity, I would have
thought. Not dutiful or respectful enough by half. Yet the
opposite was palpably true for those I allude to above. I had
missed something, clearly. What? The charming camarade-
rie that one generation can express to the other. In the
above cases, women left as widows or as single parents still
hear their names in an affectionate key.

This easy interaction across the generations occurs more normally in the way my brother recently described it. He said of his college-aged children: "I enjoy them a lot now. We are able to sit and talk about all sorts of things." Yes, I said to myself, I phoned your house, and this time your son, instead of calling you right to the phone, asked me what I was up to and chatted for a while. What a relief, I thought, to talk to them like adults. Here again I fell short, though. Why "like adults"? Why not "like friends"?

This is what we are made for as human beings – not to relate with subservience or possessiveness or overprotection or saved-up rancor, but to permit all of that to fall away so we are all on the same footing. A mother and daughter I know have clouded memories and electricity between them, yet they speak on the phone almost daily, even from different countries; the sparks still fly, yet they work pretty hard at being friends.

I have always admired the Franciscans for their appellation "Fra" or "Fray" ("Brother"), which tones down the authority-figure aspect of their priests and emphasizes the Christian family status of all in the order, to say nothing of those outside it. (The greatest "Fra" popping into my mind, however, is Dominican – Fra Angelico). Sisterly and brotherly feeling seems a charism – elusive, subject to interferences, but still of the essence.

Dante Alighieri has an instructive incident in "Purgatory," the second stage of his *Divine Comedy*. As pilgrim through the Otherworld, Dante and his guide Virgil come upon the souls expiating the capital sin of avarice, who lie face down upon the earth, bound hand and foot. Dante addresses one of them, a man who responds by confessing that he indulged this sin until late in his career as a churchman. He ended his life, but only for thirty-eight days, as a pope, Adrian V. Instinctively Dante, who elsewhere is scathing toward avarice in the church, falls to his knees in reverence. Adrian, however, sensing him closer, scolds him and tells him to get back on his feet, reminding him, "I am, like you and all the others, / a fellow servant of one Emperor" (19.137-38). In the communion, or fellowship, of saints to which we tend, the poet is telling us, we will find no hierarchy.

Our times are intent on our liberation, individually or corporately. This is the message of Freud, of Frantz Fanon (in *The Wretched of the Earth*), and of feminism in its various forms. The enduring task, though, after one achieves particularity, identity, and free space, is one of true companionship. At the end of the struggle and of the journey, we find ourselves together at our simplest before God – open-mouthed, almost, before the mystery of our existences, the intricacy of the universe, the baffling disasters of humanity, the awesomeness of a Creator. But we're reassured by the divine presence and love, which confer on us a shared identity by no means infantile – that of children of God.

REFLECTION AND ACTION

Food for Thought:

This chapter is a coda to the previous one about family feeling. Indicate to what extent the concept being proposed here, that of companionship, really registers with you.

Suggested Steps:

Try, in face of family elders, bosses, and other authority figures, not excluding pastors and bishops, to act in a companionable way. Be aware that they will not always appreciate the effort.

CHAPTER FOUR

THE HUMAN WORD AND GOD'S WORD

SONG THAT SUMS US UP

O Lord, our Lord,
how scrambled is your name
by nighttime country radios,
how faint the quasar pulse
of your receding news.
You have withdrawn your majesty
from heaven-quizzing eyes.

When we decode
the headlight beam
of galaxies
and plant our footsteps
on the backyard moon,
what is this spinoff
man
that you should search us out,
uncertain quantum
in a thronging wave?

But you pursue
this piece of cosmic junk
nudging it homeward

from an errant course.
We're told
a fireside of angels
ring it close
and deer
and dinosaurs come peering.
How is this?

O Lord, our Lord,
how kitchen near you come,
a roman candle
arching into flesh,
how many ladder steps
you struggled down,
and had old trousers on
so we could don today
your Sunday best.
(Reprinted and revised from *Signs of Life*, 1970)

When Catholic Church music in the United States got its first airing out in the 1960s, the renewed state was not altogether happy. "Mother dear, O pray for me" yielded to a succession of let's-get-together songs, many of them still with us, and confusedly romantic hymns ("I'll eat your strawberries, I'll drink your sweet wine"). "Mother dear" somehow managed to infuse its sugar into what followed. The importation of majestic Wesleyan hymns helped but did not quite strike the appropriate note for our times. Luther's "Mighty Fortress" struck a dissonant note. Fine Masses were composed by Fr. Clarence Rivers and by musicians classically trained, but their work left few traces in the songbooks.

Looking back on this enthusiastic but fiberless growth, do we find any of it mature and sturdy? Yes, we do observe at least one vigorous stem, whose roots are in the words and imagery of the psalms. It shot up mostly from Père Gelineau in France to the likes of Paul Quinlan in the United States, and thence outward into many branches and talents. Singing groups, whether seminarians or sisters, seemed to take on strength, to make a qualitative leap, when basing themselves on the psalms. We Catholics have, in other words, produced our musical version of the tree of David and kept some link, almost in spite of ourselves, with that monastic era when choirs were neither "bare" nor "ruined" and psalms were what "the sweet birds sang."

This phenomenon of our musical history, the grafting of contemporary rhythms, melody, and religious feeling upon the abiding stock of the psalms, gives witness to them once more as the world's most durable body of prayer. The psalms, in their dual quality of prayer and song, reveal themselves as the heart's outburst: "O Lord, you search me and you know me" (139); "Save me, O God, for the water comes up to my neck" (69); "How awesome are your works, O Lord" (8). They squeeze in, they concentrate, the whole religious quest and struggle. They touch upon what is most recurrent in our experience; they stir us to the depths. Singly and collectively, we tend through them toward the revealed truth of our being, with our whole equipment of heart, mind, and emotions.

What a gamut of reactions to God is run by the sayer of the psalms: open-eyed wonder of the one looking into the cosmos, a sense of how puny we are in face of this resplendent universe, a fear and trembling at the distance and apparent absence of God or at the fragility and short life of man, plus melancholy and depression and struggle towards faith and confidence in the Shepherd of Israel, as well as gratitude for any marks of providence in our family history, along with consolation and peace in the devout life.

All of this grew on me over a thirty-year period of daily return to the psalms in the Divine Office. In a recent breviary reading, I found St. Ambrose saying much the same as the above, in expanded form and glowing detail, long ago. His observations concentrate in this sentence: "In a psalm instruction vies with beauty."

The psalm form is a shining example of art capitalizing on the limits of its material, the Hebrew language – a restricted lexicon of modifiers, a slim choice of verbs, the inability of the language to form compounds – and compensating brilliantly. It does so by its parallelisms – the pairing of God's titles, the yoking of an abstract concept with a vivid particular, the expanding of initial images. It does so by its reversals of verbal position in the figure known as chiasmus – "be mine, O mountain of refuge! O fortified citadel, save me" (31). It does so, rhythmically and melodically, by its observance of a fixed number of stresses per line and by much echoing of sound within words, which moves us almost physically and heightens our response.

> O God, my God, for you I long,
> my soul ardently thirsts for you,
> my body pines for you
> More than parched earth yearns for drops of water.

The above version (and information) comes from the late Mitchell Dahood, S.J., whose long love for the psalms bore fruit in the Anchor Bible text and commentary. His introduction makes clear, in particular, the grounding of the psalms in the poetry of the pagan Ugaritic world. But he is by no means the first to have arranged and grouped the psalms, shown their place in temple cult, and traced the formation of the final collection over more than a century.

All this information helps; you can hardly learn enough about what you love. Yet most people entering the world of the psalms simply and directly, with no preparatory study, find them to express vividly what they have undergone, in darkness or light, and to be powerfully formative of their inner life. Everyone will have a different, and indeed shifting, list of favorites. (My own: 8, 33, 42, 65, 84, 91, 100, 103, 104, 126, 130, 131, 139.)

Still, and increasingly, something troubles me about the psalms these days. I seem suddenly to realize why Merton who, in *Bread in the Wilderness,* wrote so movingly of them and taught us the traditional fourfold way of praying them, felt ill at ease somehow with the psalms. I now keep noticing, perhaps under the impact of headlines from embattled zones, the prevalence in the psalms of the one word "enemy." Nelson's concordance to the New American Bible lists the incidence of "enemy" or its variant "foe" on an average of once per psalm.

The psalms seem so unforgiving. There are always enemies of the sanctuary, foes digging a pit to catch us, the taunting of the wicked. The God of Sabaoth (hosts) is "valiant in war" on behalf of the just, who are encouraged to call down thunder on their opposition. The just do not often prevail, in fact, so the psalms indulge in bemoaning and resound with continual laments. They do not seem manly in this respect. Ernesto Cardenal and Daniel Berrigan have helped me at least live with this feature of the psalms. Their paraphrases, and Berrigan's crisp commentary that accompanies his psalms in *Uncommon Prayer,* remind me how privileged we are here in the United States, our faces shiny because of special treatment. Most people in the world have great cause to wring their hands, like Tevye in *Fiddler on the Roof.* They experience firsthand that, in Berrigan's words, "the conduct of the powerful is almost invariably a mockery of God." Berrigan, and Cardenal in *The Psalms of Struggle and Liberation* (translated by Emile McAnany), make me bite my tongue as I am about to proclaim the psalms paranoid. Cardenal's version of Psalm 129, written in Nicaragua under the shadow of Somoza, rings all too true.

> From the depths I call to you Lord
> I call out in the night from prison

from the concentration camp
from the torture chamber
in the hour of darkness
hear my voice

      my S.O.S.

And Cardenal adds: "You are not implacable like them in their investigations."

Reading Berrigan's keen-edged rendition of psalms and thinking of other great versions – Mary Herbert's, Christopher Smart's – I realize that the psalms are there to challenge me and not just to be slipped into like shoes. Berrigan's concentration upon bristling images and passages is selective, intended as an antidote to "the narrow range of emotion, need, prescience, devotion, yearning" to which he sees us confining ourselves, "like a row of scrub-faced children, Sunday speeches tripping from their tongues" (p. 85). Here is a sample from Psalm 10:

Lord, why do you stand on the sidelines
silent as the mouth of the dead, the maw of the
grave –
O living One, why?. . . .
Eyes like a poniard impale the innocent
Death cheap, life cheaper. . . .
Lord, they call you blind man. Call their bluff.

Uncommon Prayer, written in the shadow of prison, never lets us forget that the way through no man's land can be hard and dry. "Still," as Berrigan says, "in a dry time on earth it is a joy to return again and again to the psalms." Yes, provided we pray them as Our Lord did (he the epitome of the pious Jew), with his readiness to forgive, his confident faith (which is, after all, the dominant motif of the psalms), the boldness of his Spirit, the sense of a universal calling. And we have to put whatever there is of us – the intense drama of the everyday, our fears and hopes for this planet

– into our own paraphrase, this true opus Dei, living by the
psalms.

REFLECTION AND ACTION

Food for Thought:
Describe the level and kind of awareness you have had
of the psalms, indicating the role they have played, or not
played, in your life.
The psalms are an epitome of Jewish prayer. May this
be said of them also as Christian prayer?

Suggested Steps:
Identify a few of your favorite psalms, noting what
makes them appeal to you.
Try paraphrasing the psalm form, filling in a familiar
text with some of your own experience. You can do this in
writing or, even better, in the context of vocal prayer.

EARTH AND SEED

> We are the earth of the word.
> From the mouth of a slung sack
> the sower scatters in an arc
> his concentrate of life.
>
> In the blizzard of influence
> upon our peculiar soil
> an inviting kernel drops
> coded to arise and unfurl.
>
> Suppose we're busy when it falls,
> or the ear's membrane is grown thick
> and friends gobble it with a laugh.
> Suppose the sleepiness of earth.

Ground of our ground, help.
If we lie smooth and hard
and a harrow alone lays open,
tremble as we may, so be.

We would flower beyond ourselves.
We would shoot up crisscross,
waving in a field,
and give back one face.

I once lived for several years in Belgium, and near us was a
field lined with family plots. Sure enough, in the sowing
season that age-old scenario of scattering the seed by hand
would be played out. I forget whether crows hovered over-
head, as in a painting by Van Gogh.

The parable of the sower is one of those jewels of
observation within easy reach yet detected only by the wise.
The uncertain fate of seeds caught the attention of Jesus
during his missionary rounds. It reminded him that his own
teaching about God's plan for the world – the kingdom of
Heaven, as he called it – was due for a very mixed reaction.
Among his influential listeners, there would be many un-
willing ears. His parables were a direct challenge to them.
"Think about it, take it home and chew on it," the teacher
as much as said.

The early church, in the person of St. Matthew and his
community, followed that advice. They mulled over the
parable of the sower, spelling it out as follows. Some people
within hearing of God's word are so hardened that it would
take a pickax to make the message penetrate. Others react
with enthusiasm when it drops but prove shallow and have
no staying power. Others attend to it seriously until their
anxieties and worldly concerns (their politics and econom-
ics) take over, choking it out. Still others, however, are
receptive and fruitful. In them God's grace can realize its

potential, on a scale from 30 to 100 percent. Happy are those who respond 100 percent.

The Holy Scriptures inevitably say to the reader, "So how about you?" For my part, I envy the people who give 100 percent – who seem to have total positive energy, no self-consciousness or self-concern or hidden agenda. I can think of a few such individuals, whose lives are a continual blessing to others. I admire too those who can sustain a depth and intensity in their service of God that seems beyond the ordinary. The saints fit here – Catherine of Siena, Martin de Porres, Ignatius of Loyola, Francis Xavier. Night or day, they fly with their whole being to God.

But a warning is in order, I think. Jesus did not intend for us to go around gauging ourselves by anybody else or measuring ourselves by some mark we cannot conceivably attain. When Jesus, in this parable, reissues the ancient message, "If today you hear God's voice, harden not your hearts" (Psalm 94), he is very much aware of his listeners. Each one is a different combination of talents, opportunities, limitations, and scars. What psychological perceptiveness he shows. The parable aims to say, for starters, "Know your resistances and watch out for them." In three deft strokes Jesus suggests the types of blockage to inspiration and grace.

The simile of the sower, on its positive side, is about generosity, openness to God. Jesus tells us, "Grace is at work in you; receive it with joy. You are precious ground – different from others maybe, needing a lot of work, but productive, full of the right ingredients. If you don't realize that, if it hasn't really dawned on you, it should."

Finally, there is the matter of the fruit, the product, of our lives. How are we to measure that? We have big plans and decided ambitions that prove so hard to realize; we have our sum of disappointments and frustrations. Are these what Jesus had in mind? Consider, though, as a counter-indication, those near-death experiences we read of from time to time. People report that in the flashbacks on their lives, what truly heartened and consoled them were the glimpses of their forgotten gestures of kindness or patience or courage and of the personal qualities they had always taken for granted.

In the last analysis there is one true measure of our lives: the extent of our configuration to Jesus Christ. How we are to embody or reflect Christ is not predetermined. It will be distinctively singular, that we can say – yet it will be authentic; it will fit in with others. The kingdom of God is a total picture, what St. Augustine called "the whole Christ." In his poem "As Kingfishers Catch Fire," Gerard Manley Hopkins expressed a field vision of the world in this condition: "Christ plays in ten thousand places, / lovely in limbs and lovely in eyes not his." This is what that hidden but immense power, God's grace, aims to produce in us.

Ours is not an age very attentive to encyclicals and long treatises. People do not seem to have the patience for them. But to crack the nut of a parable, to alter one's life thereby – that is surely an option for anyone.

REFLECTION AND ACTION

Food for Thought:

Specify where your own responses fall on the gamut of reactions to the Word of God as presented in the parable of the sower.

Ponder this prenote to the *Spiritual Exercises* of St. Ignatius Loyola: "It will be very profitable for the one who is to go through the Exercises to enter upon them with magnanimity and generosity toward one's Creator and Lord and to offer one's entire will and liberty."

Suggested Steps:

Take advantage of the helps available to enter into Our Lord's parables, such as Joachim Jeremias (*The Parables of Jesus*), the Sacra Pagina series of commentaries on the gospels of St. Matthew and St. Luke, *The New Jerome Biblical Commentary*, etc.

Make sure to choose a good patron saint, one whom you admire for qualities that are within your range or walk of life, allowing always for your own combination of health, opportunities, graces, and limitations.

WISEWRITER

> Faith is a gambling man,
>   he stakes all his chips.
>
> Faith is a calm
>   for many a tossing ship.

The early days of word processing gave rise to one especially beguiling program, Easywriter. Here, presumably, was a life belt for the floundering freshman or the newly promoted boss. Of course, no one was about to be fooled. Quick skill is a contradictory notion. Anyone conscientious about writing – novice or old pro – will keep a weather eye out for models and helps and will turn gratefully to spell checkers and style rectifiers in the tradition of Grammatik III and Write Right. But correctness and standard technique do not of themselves amount to adequate form, to the living word.

Those of us in the 1990s trying to inscribe some religious insight into our social commentaries, our ethical reasoning, our probing of psychology, our exegeses, our homilies, face a continuing question: How can the word of God be presented alive? One sort of clue to an answer lies

in the direction of the old teachers of the Hebrew Bible –
Ben Sirach (the author of Ecclesiasticus), Qoheleth (the
author of Ecclesiastes), and the compiler of Proverbs. These
spokesmen for the mysterious realm called "wisdom" were,
after all, accorded a sacred standing, along with the compilers of the Torah and the great prophets.

> Listen, my son, and take my advice;
> > refuse not my counsel.
> Put your feet into the snare of wisdom
> > and your neck into her noose.
> Stoop your shoulders to carry her
> > and do not be irked at her bonds.
> > (Ecclesiasticus 6:24-6)

Let yourselves be caught by wisdom, says the scribe,
with the freshness, and even the slight shock of surprise,
requisite to a decent metaphor. There is a nutshell concentration to the wisdom saying that lodges it in the receptive
mind. "Let your acquaintances be many, / but one in a
thousand your confidant" (Ecclus. 6:5). "A discerning man
talks sense, / but the senseless needs a stick to his back"
(Prov. 10:12). This nondiscursive manner of teaching and
thinking is validated by a couplet from Ben Sirach: "The
mind of a sage appreciates proverbs; to the attentive ear,
wisdom is a joy" (Ecclus. 3:28).

The Jews were not the first to crystallize their hard-won
insights, along with their worldly-wise caveats, into a pithy
form, and then to collect them. Most peoples before or since
have recognized that their language is at its best in these
quasi-poetic formulae, notable for shortness, sense, and salt.
English is certainly full of them: "dead men tell no tales,"
"the chickens have come home to roost," "a new broom
sweeps clean." My mother and aunts raised us children on
the shrewdness of Italian proverbs, some of them smacking
of Poor Richard in their exhortations to thrift and industry,
some too having a marvelous savor. I have sometimes la-

bored to translate them, but the concision and the rhythmic balance of the originals keep slipping away: "*Fra moglie e marito non metteci il dito*" ("Don't stick your nose between husband and wife"), "*Sacco vuoto non sta in piedi*" ("An empty sack cannot stand up"), "*Chi non mangia ha gia mangiato*" ("The one who won't eat has eaten").

Jesus, clearly, was nourished on the wisdom tradition. Consider his familiar appeal: "Take my yoke upon you, and learn from me; . . . For my yoke is easy and my burden light" (Matt. 11:29-30). Does this not echo the passage from Ecclesiasticus about stooping one's shoulders to carry wisdom? Jesus was alert to the contrastive colors of wisdom writing, its systematic juxtaposition of the alert disciple and the utter fool. To willfully reject wisdom is to spell one's doom. The Psalms too capitalized on this strong contrast. The very opening of the psalter says that the one whose "delight is in the law of the Lord . . . is like a tree planted by streams of water, that yields its fruit in due season." The wicked are "like chaff which the wind drives away" (Ps. 1:34). Jesus, in the course of proposing the kingdom to his listeners as a crucial choice, paints it often in these stark oppositions:

> Everyone who hears these words of mine and does them will be like a wise man who built his house upon the rock, and the rain fell, and the floods came, and the winds blew and beat upon that house, but it did not fall, because it had been founded on the rock. And everyone who hears these words of mine and does not do them will be like a foolish man who built his house upon the sand. (Matt. 7:24-26)

Jesus purified all he touched, including his people's proverbs. The Beatitudes are an exalted and paradoxical reversal of the worldly wisdom that slips even into the pages ascribed to Solomon. "Blessed are the poor in spirit," the very first line in St. Matthew's summary of his teaching, sets something straight that is still wavery in the Wisdom books.

In a more general way, it may be said of the teaching of Jesus that his vividness, drawn from sharp observation of his surroundings and from rumination on local events, is what makes the gospels such food for thought, line by line. In the Byzantine church, when the deacon marches to the lectern with the gospel book, chanting "Wisdom," we know what he refers to.

Mother Teresa has caught the storytelling power of Jesus, his way of embodying crucial truths in specifics, with her own almost formulaic refrain: "A man came to our house." This opening has alerted her hearers, by the thousands, to some miracle of providence, some evidence of God's care for the desperate, some encouragement to trust God completely. The Hebrew literature of wisdom was addressed by males to males in the scribal schools. For all their warnings against the enticements of "the strange woman" and the noninclusivity of their language, Ben Sirach, Qoheleth, and the author of Proverbs did give to Wisdom a feminine persona, thereby stirring the disciples to a passionate attachment. This personification of Wisdom as feminine has been actualized over and over – in Hildegard of Bingen, the abbess Hilda of Whitby, Saint Gertrude, Catherine of Siena, Teresa of Avila, and, skipping many, to come to our own era, in Simone Weil, Dorothy Day, Gertrude Von le Fort.

The wisdom language, it must be said, has much to contend with in a milieu that equates learning with analytic procedure – categorizing, distinguishing and subdividing, explaining, using inferences to draw a conclusion. And who can plausibly deny that on the way to understanding, to illumination, this kind of systematic process is crucial, inescapable? Still, when all is said and done, the true power of our statements about the holy – about our service to God and our commitment to one another – comes from the paradoxical and the pithy and the experiential.

The fascinating thing about the Hebrew wisdom tradition is that it carried its own deconstructive pages – its own self-deflating, or at least self-correcting, texts – Ecclesiastes and Job. If Proverbs and Ecclesiasticus preach a moral assurance and a contemplative vision of created order, the compilers of the Bible were honest enough to include Ecclesiastes, which seems to undercut the establishment of any kingdom, any perfect community, on earth. We read in chapter 1: "The sun rises and the sun sets . . . Everything has its season . . . There is nothing new under the sun." In this "strangest book in the Bible," as the introduction of the Anchor Bible puts it, God seems a "mysterious, inscrutable being," and our efforts very transitory indeed. The Psalms too give us sudden reminders of how precarious life is: "You turn people back into dust, . . . / You sweep them away like a dream" (Ps. 70); we are "merely a breath," and our "life fades like a shadow" (Ps. 144). Ecclesiastes says this in a systematic way. Yet the courage with which its pre-Christian writer "affirms life's values in the teeth of its brevity and frustrations" (again according to the Anchor Bible) is itself a discipline and a moral encouragement to those whose best efforts are hindered by illness or their own failings or an intractable environment.

The aphoristic spirit of wisdom literature inscribes its own contradiction, by way of a marvelous irony, in the book of Job. This book of the Old Testament begins and ends in a storytelling mode, but all the rest is an elaborate debate. The style is expansive, oratorical, and florid – but so, after all, were the showpiece passages praising Wisdom in Proverbs and Ecclesiasticus. The reader gets not so much a message as a dialectic. The progress and tenor of Job is summed up in the Anchor Bible's introduction:

> A man of exemplary rectitude and piety is suddenly overwhelmed with disasters and loathsome disease. How can such a situation be reconciled with divine justice

and benevolent providence? It must be admitted first and last that the book of Job fails to give a clear and definitive answer to this question. Virtually every basic argument, however, that has been adduced in connection with the problem is touched on. (p. lxxiii)

The complete evasion of the issue as Job had posed it must be the poet's oblique way of admitting that there is no satisfactory answer available to man, apart from faith: "God cannot be summoned like a defendant and forced to bear witness against himself" (p. lxxx).

The book of Job is a chastening reminder that wisdom admits of many styles. There is nothing exactly sacred about the aphoristic way, the pithy expression. On the other hand, it is hard to exaggerate how much a reader welcomes such a tendency in a writer, and how effective it is for embodying the word. So, fellow scribes, my homiletic sisters and brothers – if I may indulge in the personal and exhortatory, with Ben Sirach and the author of Proverbs as my models – may our words be affected by these powerful examples. Let their spirit of wise writing enter us.

REFLECTION AND ACTION

Food for Thought:

Among sayings of the Gospels and of the Hebrew wisdom writings, pick and list some that are readily applicable to yourself.

Suggested Steps:

From your own life and experience, try composing some wisdom sayings.

THE ELECT ARE CALLED TO HEAVEN

1.
as if fresh from volleyball
    both sexes
sandy-haired
of a height, an age
(family resemblance
    notable)
nude because it's June
    and the Renaissance
mole, cicatrix, or tatoo
    none
their pectorals
    pronounced
pick of the species
Luca Signorelli pinxit

2.
in a Manhattan headwind
the year-end composer
    (fumbling at the ideal)
assembles
the wigged lady
    (tennies but no socks)
the Rolex merchants
    stern, with attaché case
youth in a Yankee cap
    backwards
heads of Medusa hair
or of hair expertly coiffed
a pitchman from India
    "good price! good
        price!"
baby in stroller behind

clear plastic
good-natured looney
    (we're on his steps)
arm-in-arm Asians
    puzzled
some health-club specimens
    (sneaking a smoke)
runts, feed-sack bodies
and two that lean on
        crutches

hold still, everyone
think paradise
yes, that's it (flash)
perfect

Art and religious faith are two passions, and passions make rigorous demands. Is there room enough for them both in one life? That depends on how much energy you have. After all, life has always to contain competing demands – business and home, friendship and romance, sports and relatives. Maturity means getting our priorities straight.

God and creativity seem like an easy match, a natural. In actuality, it isn't at all simple. God is a consuming fire. "My son, give me your heart" ("My daughter, give me all your attention"), God asks the divinity student (Prov. 23, 26). Does this mean don't give it to the stage, don't give it to jazz, don't give it to storytelling?

The call to discipleship is radical. "Sell what you have, give it to the poor, and come follow me," Jesus insists. "Unless you deny yourself and take up your cross, you cannot be my disciple." This does not seem to leave room for the day-dreaming ("sleep of the soul" Maritain calls it), the self-awareness, the expenditure of time and precious materials – the necessary wastage, in other words – of art. Of course, neither does it seem to allow for romance, with so many larks and dead ends, or for bank accounts or financial planning, or for a regime of athletics. But let's concentrate on art.

Gerard Manley Hopkins, as a young Jesuit in Victorian England, thought that following a religious vocation meant the necessary sacrifice of his art, his precious poetry. For another whole century, after all, seminary and convent life would convey precisely that expectation. Concert pianists, budding sculptors, to say nothing of aspiring writers, would find, upon entering religion, that they had to put their art on the back burner, giving it sporadic attention but never the absorbing interest and fierce dedication requisite for art.

Hopkins, entering religion, thought of his poetry as an indulgence of the ego incompatible with a humble life, a life centered on God. It took a religious superior, eventually – his seminary rector – to step in when Hopkins was marveling at a newspaper report of Christian heroism and to tell him directly, "God wants you to write about it." Then the dam burst. All the imagery and insight and intense feeling that he had been storing up for years broke into one tremendous artistic expression of faith, "The Wreck of the Deutschland."

It would be wrong to dismiss the early feelings of Hopkins as rigoristic and neurotic – "pre-Vatican II." Hopkins had also sensed something quite true: that the priorities have to be declared and assured, sometimes at a high cost. One thinks of Mary Lou Williams, who abandoned jazz piano and composition after her Catholic conversion, only to go back and compose her powerful *Mass* years later. Hopkins, at the start, staked out his total offering. But then, like Abraham, he was ready for a theological lesson not in his textbooks: that the verb *to sacrifice* does not mean primarily "to destroy" but "to make holy," to offer God something dear to us. That incredible gift for vivid, musical language, for a punchy kind of rhythm and a syntax all his own, was *the* offering for which we now revere Gerard Manley Hopkins. His poetry was a unique outlet for his genuine devotion, for his neurotic but very pure spirit and intense affection. Talents and gifts have that purpose, to flower for God. It is what we owe ourselves and God. "Something beautiful for God" is not just about the life of Mother Teresa and about ministering to the homeless.

The illustrator and engraver Fritz Eichenberg, a Quaker, was drawn magnetically to Dorothy Day. His block engravings of Christ among the poor, and his cartoons about injustice, were inspired by what he learned from her and saw at the Catholic Worker house. In the introduction to a book of his drawings, *Works of Mercy*, Jim Forest, an ex-volunteer, says: "Fritz, in his modesty, considered his own contributions to be relatively minor compared to the heroic feats of those who lived among the destitute or went to prison in pursuit of peace." Yet the Eichenberg engravings, especially "Christ of the Breadlines" and "Black Crucifixion," are what people remember best – indelibly, we might say – about *The Catholic Worker*.

How about the conflicts, the facets of art and faith that seem averse to one another, contradictory? Sensuous receptivity and ascetic Christianity do not make easy roommates. Take the case of Manuel de Falla, perhaps Spain's greatest composer of this century, a bachelor and an intensely religious man. De Falla, oddly, wrote nothing in the genre of sacred music. His most famous composition is *El Amor Brujo* (*That Witching Love*), a dramatization, or orchestration, of Eros. Later he repudiated that work, felt guilty for having composed it, probably confessed it, and stipulated in his will (too late, fortunately) that it be performed no more.

We can admire such strength of will, such resolute character. De Falla was not just being silly, "impossibly Spanish." *El Amor Brujo*, after all, is a force, a passion among the strongest, that absorbs and overwhelms and makes a plaything of conscience and reason. Yet we can also admire the music, which has nothing at all pandering or seductive about it; it catches an elemental truth.

Friedrich von Schiller, the great German Romantic, was perhaps not wrong to say, "Excruciating honesty and total freedom from restraint is what we find nowhere else but in authentic works of art." The restraint, or constraint, I think, has to come from within, from our way of seeing things. Does what you write or depict or sculpt have the mark of a believer? That is by no means a simple question. Ask Cezanne. The mere subject matter does not supply an answer. Some people handle religious subjects, even for a lifetime, without much depth; others treat the creaturely world, the so-called secular, with great reverence. Is it art or faith that is lacking in the first case and that triumphs in the second?

It is our faith, is it not, that will determine how we register things, that will give us a certain way of feeling and seeing. Saint Ignatius of Loyola, at the culmination of his *Spiritual Exercises*, urges us to look at everything surrounding us and precious to us as streaming down from the love of God to each one personally. He entitles this exercise "Contemplation for Obtaining Love" and intends that it permeate our daily life.

Our experience, on the other hand, the skein of our lives, will serve up the subject matter, the unformed substance of our art. Experience can be cruel and painful, as well as happy. Roberta Nobleman, an English-born actor and teacher, developed a series of one-woman shows focused on women of faith – Julian of Norwich, Mary of Nazareth, Teresa of Avila, Jeanette Piccard. Eventually this woman of faith and of the theater had to face, to assume as subject matter, the trauma of her own early life: her childhood experience of incest with her father. Thanks to confrontation, continual prayer (she is an active Episcopalian), and years of therapy, she had passed from victim to survivor, and then to a more peaceful condition. But her hurt and healing were still in need of a "celebrant," as she put it.

Roberta Nobleman achieved this in *Masks and Mirrors*, a dramatic collage meant for inclusion within a workshop or discussion setting. Nobleman intertwines her own story (five years of abuse relieved by exciting visits to the theater) with that of Virginia Woolf, who was abused by her two half-brothers and who took refuge in story writing, and with that of Gustav Mahler, whose painful but serene *Resurrection Symphony* she plays as background to a difficult sequence. *Masks and Mirrors*, as the title promises, is profuse in the symbolic. Most touching are the child masks, which are worn for mimed episodes, most haunting is the male mask of the sad-sack abuser, a scarred man who is mimed as wielding his power. At one point the actress brings out a barrel of avoidance objects, a humorous litter; at another she performs the Scottish ballad "Tam Lin," an allegorical romance about the phases of hurt and healing. Plays by women on the subject of violation have commanded most of the attention this year (1993) at the Humana Festival of New American Plays at Louisville, Kentucky. Nobleman has made her strong and positive contribution to this current concern.

An art is a passion in that it makes one ferociously exact about detail, it allows a wide range of freedom ("Here are the materials; go to it"), and it brings the artisan, the craftsman, great satisfaction and joy. Dabbling is fine – occasional gardening, decorating, sketching, or sitting down at the piano. But a hobby or craft becomes an art and a passion (imperceptibly, no doubt) when you think about it a lot, when you study how others have done it, when you try out many styles and forms, with the inevitable dead ends, on the way to developing your own voice, your own signature.

I have been serious about poetry since writing Christmas verse as a child. At school and in seminary I was given many opportunities to study it, though not so many to write it. In graduate school and as a college English teacher I got more latitude, more encouragement – not much more time, but I became more resolute in stealing it. Poetry Writing was the most successful of my courses because it tapped the creativity and the sensitivity of students in an unusual way. And it kept my own juices flowing.

Living now in New York, I find myself gaping continually at the profusion of life about me on the streets, not much of it conforming to any standard. Recently, looking through art books for depictions of heaven or paradise, I was struck by a Renaissance vision of that happy place, *Gli Eletti Sono Vocati al Cielo* (*The Elect Are Called to Heaven*). The Renaissance had a definite bodily ideal, which the streets of New York contradict at every turn. Whether New York is to any extent a heaven, diversity is a fact of life here; it is long past the stage of slogan. Hence the poem I include with these ponderings.

REFLECTION AND ACTION

Food for Thought:

If there are competing passions in your life, admit it here and explain what you do about it – whether you dovetail them, reconcile them, keep the priority clear between them, compromise between them, or find yourself pulled apart by absorbing interests.

Suggested Steps:

According to your own talents, interests, perhaps artistry, do "something beautiful for God."

CHAPTER FIVE

ATTITUDE TO THINGS
OF THIS WORLD

IMPEDIMENTS

The heroism of snails, house on back!
I am terrified of my baggage, sitting smack center
in a rash of books, crating. What can I do without?
The answer's piddling. Also I sack up
wool sweaters, sweatclothes, slacks, stitched
shirts, a London Fog coat. No fabric
lacks. And a clog of pennies,
pins, pencils, stubs, rubber bands. Dust
everywhere; coughing racks me, or a split
head. What mounds of paper! The pulp mills
turning jack pine into the *Chronicle*, the *Monitor*,
heap me in stained leaves. Urgent
and official letters have been lost track.
Only a fanatic with tweezer probe
layer through layer could crack
their mystery. I sit reading,
shredding. The mess thickens. I close my eyes.
Goods come for transportation, on and on.
I pine for the knack. I recall
tottering into woods with the essentials
squeezed into one pack.

Late August of last year found me sitting on the floor in my room in Nobili Hall, Santa Clara University, sorting out. I wanted to cull the superfluous from my eight file drawers rather than lug the lot across the country to New York City. I might have saved myself some trouble with a more radical solution, because about a third of the prized files, crated precariously, never made it through the U.S. mail. But I was in no frame of mind to cut so sharply. Such is the much-feared process known as moving.

Thirty boxes eventually followed me, at their own pace, to New York. I was stunned, and still am, by the sheer volume of my essentials. I had, after all, redistributed about half of my books and carried box upon box of detritus – old *New Yorkers,* newsletters, promotional materials, catalogs, worn shirts and slippers, medicines barely touched – to the dumpster. I left behind framed pictures, backpacking equipment, and toiletries abundant. Yet I went off with a baggage train of thirty boxes! To tell the full truth, I was a few hours short of finishing when the hour of departure struck, and I rushed off to the airport, leaving the cleanup operation to the monks at Santa Clara.

This experience of sheer accumulation unsettled me. It seemed to knock into a cocked hat all pretensions to religious poverty. From where I write now, in fact, I look down from a ninth-story window upon one of the homeless who has lived for several years outside our building. When she wants to go anywhere or get out of a coming rainstorm, she packs up a couple of neat bundles and is off. That's poverty; it is also selectivity and desperate determination. As for me, the pile is mounting again. What a trial I would have posed, I sometimes reflect, to any tidy roommate, for example a wife.

During the countdown hours at Santa Clara, one of the pages I came upon was my poem "Impediments," written for a previous migration. I like the word "impediments" because of its Latin root, *impedimenta,* meaning baggage, things that weigh heavy on a march. (The poem can be dated somewhat from the fact that the *Monitor,* San Francisco's archdiocesan newspaper, ceased publication about 1983.) Upon rereading my own words, my eyes went wide, not just at the identical parade of details but at the identical feelings expressed on an earlier date. Our lives do provide us with continual reruns of our most embarrassing moments.

A more recent episode figures in my musings. On the third Sunday of Advent, finishing Mass in a women's prison facility, I set out to distribute a number of Christmas cards that had been donated for the inmates. There was a generous supply – cards of six or seven different designs, enough of each for everybody. Alas, the various cards were intermixed, and Sister Carmela, whom I assist, was not present that day to ensure their orderly distribution. So, after a peaceful liturgy, chaos broke out among the two dozen or so women as they clamored to reach for one card of each type. The guard on duty had to move in to disperse the group, which had entirely gotten the better of me.

Afterward, back home, I wondered aloud what had happened. One of the brethren helped me with this reflection. "To the poor," he said – and who poorer than the incarcerated – "every slightest possession is highly important." Thus he made sense of their eagerness – the same eagerness I have found among inmates, Catholic or not, to have and wear multiple rosaries. I was getting a glimpse of the symbolic role of objects to us in our fleshly state. Along with what is strictly useful, we treasure what gives us some meaning or worth. It is part of human dignity to have things of one's own.

Nonetheless, I cannot help admitting, for myself, as someone pledged to an evangelical way of life, how large is my inventory. If the evangelist, by definition and as opposed to the settled minister, is one who travels light – like the

Son of Man, with "no place to lay his head" (Luke 9, 58) –
then I have probably lost the knack. Does Jesus Christ fail
to recognize me as one of his mobile ones? A daunting
thought. Does he understand that I need all those books?
A poser for the first world.

Thoreau's old cry of "Simplicity! Simplicity! Simplicity!" is certainly hard to honor in the land of plenty. When
missionaries return to the United States from abroad, they
are overwhelmed by the sheer quantity of available stock.
One of them, back on a breather after years with Salvadoran
refugees, remarked about American advertising and all-pur-
pose stores: "What an immense amount of stuff they can get
people to want!" True. A local high school teacher added
the following: "Young people growing up are used to so
much. How hard for them to be unselfish."

De te fabula, I tell myself, "The lesson's for you." Don't
worry so much about teenagers.

REFLECTION AND ACTION

Food for Thought:

Reflect on your own habits of collecting; that is, measure how much control you have over it. Neatness enters into
this topic as a guard against getting bogged down with
"stuff."

As I write this, people are fleeing their homes in north-
ern California in the face of flood waters. Imagine, in such
a circumstance, what you would find essential to save.

Suggested Steps:

Make that trip to the dumpster, to the Salvation Army,
or to Goodwill that excess may call for.

Pray, in realistic terms, over this matter and over the
image of simplicity that the gospel can project for our times.

RESCUE OF CITY THINGS

I am the light of the city,
a crack of green on the gray block.

I am a glint to contradict
any designs of knife upon

I burn through the exhaust of sundown,
and join the watch over neighborhoods.

Strike me, I ask, into dark pockets
where the old have none to jingle against.

Proceed with me as a plain candle
into the nightglare hurtful to late stars.

What if no rooster be allowed to crow!
I can still dawn out of the sleepless.

Living in the city takes a lot out of you. Perhaps I should
not talk, having passed my adult life under lesser compres-
sion, in those greener tracts known as the suburbs. Still,
besides having some extended experience of San Francisco,
I am just now finishing four months in Mexico City, which
should count for something.

In Mexico City I have seen wear and tear on my students
from traffic snarls, close encounters with theft or assault,
depression (their own or that of friends), and government
takeover of properties (to build low-cost housing). The remarkable thing is, in fact, people's resilience. Since the 1985
earthquake, at all events, and the rise of pollution to record
levels, the quality of life, or concern about how to improve
it, has been a constant topic in *la Capital*. Mexican writers
have been giving their major city this attention for some
time. Jose Carlos Becerra wrote in 1976:

This city hurts me,
it hurts me, for its progress falls heavy on me
like an invincible dead man;
it is like eternity asleep with its back turned
to all of my questions.

Salvador Novo, looking out in the morning, imagined this: "A white soapy foam floats in the watery sky." Enrique Gonzalez Rojo identified the city with "houses of thirty stories, architectural wasp nests." (One of these nests, part of a development in Tlaltelolco, came down in the 1985 earthquake.) Jaime Labastida, underlining the division between those who profit and those who pay dearly in our "sumptuous cities, those solemn chatterboxes," noted the continual danger: "We are living cruel times/and have to keep our eye out for/the remorseless man with axe in hand/as if he's crossing a forest." Finally, Efrain Huerta emerged in the past generation as a dyed-in-the-wool Chilango (Mexico City resident, joshed for consumption of chili), a reciter of street names and rider of buses in this city "one is enamored of – there's no remedy for it." Huerta, who wrote a "Declaration of Love" to the capital, also found himself driven to a stinging "Declaration of Hate":

City so complicated, boiling pot of envies,
breeding ground of virtues undone in an hour,
a nest each of us occupies like a burning word ignored,
surface we cross in an obscure passage,
desert where we breathe vices out and in,
a dense wood rained upon by sad and piercing tears.

Huerta seems to bear out the claim of his contemporary Ali Chumacero that "the poet is a sad man, disconsolate at heart." Yet more fairly we can discover in him, purely and simply, a man sensitive to the totality of things round about – what the French called, making the preposition into a noun, environment. Anyone who has tried, after all, knows how hard it is to get one's thoughts together in the city.

One has the sense of being jostled through life. "In my city," said Mariangeles Comesana, "where itchiness runs from pole to pole,/and the trees have lost the language of birds,/I have learned to throb without let-up" ("City Gray Hen"). A period of prayer or reflection is likely to have, for background noise, the gunning of motors, impatient horns, car alarms going off, if not the slamming of doors, arguments, or heavy music through thin walls.

Of course, human beings started heaping together a long time ago, with precious few of the conveniences we now take for granted. But whereas some things hugely improve, others get grimmer. Ignatius of Loyola loved to go out late onto the roof of the Jesuit college in Rome to contemplate the stars. LeRoi Jones (now Imamu Amiri Baraka fighting to improve his home city of Newark) put the heavenly prospect in terms more familiar to modern city folk: "And now each night I count the stars,/ And each night I get the same number." A mere handful, of course, and often "they will not come to be counted." The grim humor of city life is in his title: "Preface to a Twenty-Volume Suicide Note."

What with the drift of grime about us and the rundown look so omnipresent, it is hard to stop, look, admire, praise. It is hard to translate into big-city daily experience the conviction of Rainer Maria Rilke, early in this century, that "to be here is much, and the transient Here/seems to need and concern us strangely. Us, the most transient." Rilke devoted the ninth of his *Duino Elegies* to insisting that we bear a responsibility to the objects among which our life is set. Not that we are to define ourselves by the possession of "things," but rather to elicit from ourselves a respect for things. This is the kind of reverence for creatures, precisely, that Ignatius of Loyola proposes as the "Principle and Foundation" to his *Spiritual Exercises.*

The trouble with all our absorption in projects and tasks, according to Rilke, is that "more than ever/ the things that we can live by are falling away,/supplanted by an action without symbol," deeds without any depth. He warned also against the withdrawal tactic of spiritualism; he warned, that is, against going to dwell on some exalted plane rather than taking interest in "the simple thing that is shaped in passing from father to son,/that lives near our hands and eyes as our very own." What is it that passes on thus, and improves along the way? Palpable things that we tend, or upon which we can exercise our skills, giving shape, repairing – plant life, wood, food, fabrics, machinery, circuitry. This is the material on which the earthly imagination works.

In the dreariest parts of the city, people have given up trying to put an appealing face on things; the objects of business or the home surroundings are treated offhandedly, even roughly. The cleanup people, those unsung city heroes, never seem to penetrate to these sectors. Yet even the objects with a grimy face, including those that we synthesize from chemicals, are making their appeal – for careful handling, imagination, and even more, a kind of reverence:

> . . . these things that live,
> slipping away, understand that you praise them;
> transitory themselves, they trust us for rescue.
> . . . They wish us to transmute them
> in our invisible heart. . .
> Earth, isn't this what you want: *invisibly*
> to arise in us?

Rilke accepted this charge: "Earth, dear one, I will!" True, he wrote this at a time when his friends offered him lodging in the country, away from the afflicted urban masses. Still, he broaches to everyone the challenge to be contemplative in the very hive of busyness – to subordinate one's anxiety about upward mobility, or success in projects, or merely surviving, to the appreciative use of eyes and an imaginative handling of the ordinary.

One thinks here instinctively of Teilhard de Chardin, who loved the earth intensely and did live for long periods in the great urban centers – Paris, Peking, New York (where he died on Easter, 1955). Teilhard vowed himself to the earth from youth, with an earnestness that shocked some people and sounded pagan to them. These people quite mistook Teilhard, as Father Henri de Lubac was constantly at pains to point out. De Lubac would have us notice Teilhard twice quoting a favorite mystic, St. Angela of Foligno, and commenting, "St. Angela saw that every creature is full of God." Father Teilhard, de Lubac said, "translates this classic teaching into his language, speaking of that 'universal transparency' to the eyes of faith which for him constitutes the 'divine milieu.'"

Teilhard had a vision, which he expressed daringly in "Messe sur le Monde." He saw the earth, transparent with Christ, becoming as it were Eucharistic. Central to this vision, as we learn from other works of his, was the unity, or unification, of peoples over the surface of the planet, the inevitability of a kind of world-city. We shudder at the thought; he would accuse us of little faith. He was convinced that the more complex our organizations, the greater the chances for human awareness and development.

Actually, for many people, life in the city produces euphoria, excitement. They are charged with its energies, grateful for its multiple resources. They are bored anywhere else. May their genuine optimism not blunt their awareness of the terrible wear and tear on so many fellow citizens. Teilhard himself knew quite well the resistances of matter and that city living is marked deeply with the cross – the very sign that we can imagine people making these days for protection as they go down into the subway.

Teilhard felt a pressing call to work for the success of the world; he found this call implicit in the petition of the Our Father, "thy kingdom come." For Teilhard, the success of the world had a real tie both to preparing and to reflecting the kingdom of God. He thought of this planet – and especially of its cities, we may say – as the stuff for a metamorphosis. From this milieu new heavens, a new earth, may emerge.

As we think of our urban conglomerates and their chaos, the chances for transformation seem dim. But we start where we find ourselves, which means often enough as irreversibly city people. As Labastida put it, "The city is in me, the city which erases me and writes me." And Alexander Aura said, "No way to retract a foot/so as to forget the city./It holds me for good,/I am its vice." Vicente Quirarte, speaking directly to the city in "A Eulogy for the Street," expressed our ambiguous relationship with it as happening this way: to fling down finally in a chance hotel our being, tired out with existence, and just as our muscles and eyelids are capitulating, still to remember you and love you, even after the battle, even though tomorrow, waking up again, we ask: "Here we are, city, and why the devil?"

So we want, or should want, to foster and to put our own touch on the creatures around us, those that move and those that stay still. We want to make our surroundings the matter of our praise, almost in spite of themselves. If this often means taking initiative in the face of sullen resistance, and we do not know where the courage will come from, we have these chiding but also impelling words from one who promised to be present for all eventualities, "O you of little faith."

Note: The translation of Rilke is by C. F. Macintyre in *The Duino Elegies*, University of California Press, 1963. The sources for Teilhard de Chardin are *The Prayer of Teilhard de Chardin,* Henri de Lubac, S.J., chapter 4, and *Un Prophète en Proces: Teilhard de Chardin,* René d'Ouince, S.J., volume 2. For the city poetry of Mexico, I am indebted to Professor Manuel Muñoz Aguado of the Universidad Iberoamericana, and to his students. The translations are mine.

REFLECTION AND ACTION

Food for Thought:
     To be contemplative in the hive of busyness – indicate what success you have had in doing that.
     Spell out your attitude about city life today, the extent to which you have, or do not have, faith in something salvific happening there.

Suggested Steps:
     Engage yourself in the city environment in some help-ful way, if you can. Assist these often grim surroundings to somehow lift the spirit and yield praise of God.

HAVING SOME WORDS WITH MARTHA

     The invitations said
     "Banquet at seven,
     French food and dancing,
     please, please come."
     And I was going
     when the committee broke,
     after the roll calls,
     minutes,
     motions on the table,
     hands,
     word wrangles,
     recounts,
     huddles and strategies.
     They sent a messenger:

"The band has struck up
and champagne is foaming,
all the guests have come.
There's quiche and sweetbreads."
That was fine with me.
But first
ah, first
a few questionnaires –
Do you approve of X?
In the hypothesis of Y
should we do Z?
Please take your time,
careful,
we count on you.

A phone call came:
"We're bolting the front doors-
freeloaders crashing!
You can get in the back,
but hurry."
Sure. O.K. Soon as
I write up the reports,
get a few letters out
postmarked no later than today,
after an interview or two,
a memo,
some few calls returned.
When I can rip this page
out of my office calendar,
I'm there.

Meanwhile, please
put a warm plate aside.

I composed the accompanying poem at a hectic moment in 1972. How much has changed since then? One guess. No, the Law of Acceleration has lost none of its prominence among the laws of nature, whereas I am still all ears for any law of deceleration. One learns about breakdown, of course, major or minor, but breakdown is hardly among the normal impulses of life or purposes of the Creator.

The reality of living at high speed these days – the famous American Way – impinges variously. I myself imagine a bit of conversation. *Question:* What did you last watch on television? *Answer:* If I remember correctly, the Super Bowl. Or consider the dream a friend recently recounted. She had six visits to make in half an hour, all during peak traffic. That's when you wake up tired! My department chairman speaks of the sensation of never catching up. I have at times had an almost surrealist sense of things literally flying by, and I waving at them as they go.

The implication here, of course, is nonengagement with the passing time, heavy as one's agenda may actually be. I have enjoyed jogging, over the years, for the reason that it gets the world going at my pace for a short period daily. More recently, choral singing has become my special recreation because a concert, or even a good rehearsal, gives me such a positive and productive sense (and my glitches are swallowed into the larger euphony).

A long while back, in the seminary, our mentor gave us the Latin adage *Non multa sed multum* – Not a lot of things but much of some one thing. My experience in past years has been too often the opposite: *Non multum sed multa.* That puts me among the Marthas to whom Jesus was speaking in his memorable conversation with the sister of contemplative Mary: "Martha, Martha, you are worked up about a lot of things; only one is really essential."

Poor Martha. Puts herself out a hundred percent, and what does she get? A scolding. Much indeed can be said in

Martha's defense. Where, for instance, did Jesus and his disciples think lunch was coming from? But it would all be beside the point. While tending, she was not attending, not centered. Her action did not grow from any contemplative root, any awareness of her being in the presence of and in close bond with the divine. She did not have the right perspective. Do we have any proof of that? Her anger, her anxiety.

As I try talking further sense to myself on this subject, a few guidelines appear. I assure myself, first of all, that it is not evil to be busy, even superbusy. Needless guilt feelings are no help in sorting out what we can undertake and what we cannot. A pastoral vocation, a human-services calling, seems by its nature to postulate a varied rather than a concentrated life. That is why in the Catholic university there is some, often much, inevitable tension between scholarly production and pastoral action. We read of Jesus being surrounded by the crowds and so concerned with responding to these "lost sheep" as barely to have time to eat. But he knew that his exertions were no guarantee of fruitfulness; he was saddened but not unstrung by meager results. And he stayed fully in union with his Father, even if it meant sometimes sneaking away.

Beginning as we do then with *élan*, a generous impulse, how is it that we end up so often depleted and swamped? The trouble comes, clearly, from some failure to recognize or accept limits. The reluctance to give up something, especially something of one's own devising, or to seem other than omnipotent, will surely bring on overload, the panicky feeling that the central exchange has more calls coming in than one can handle. From overload comes anger and depression, because you cannot accomplish what you would wish, or exhaustion, because you strive doggedly to do so anyway. Meanwhile, some poor, unwitting soul phones in and gets the sharp edge of your voice, without any idea why.

Dialogue takes place continually, I think, between one's physical energies and one's emotions or attitudes. If one has a relish for what one is doing, that supplies tremendous energy; it elicits maximum collaboration from the body. Jesus must have labored thus, looking uniquely to the purpose his Father had proposed to him. He, too, tired out, of course, and had to take his repose. If, in addition, a person nurses resentment of some kind, or suffers from excessive self-concern (overdramatizes, perhaps, and I should talk!), this constitutes a drain on the system before one even begins a task. It is like driving with the brake on.

We, recognizing how much anxiety, irritability, or hypersensitivity will manage to seep in amid our good will and our most generous impulses, will want to keep clearing the focus and also, as we choose our tasks and projects, to have constant recourse to the great virtue of prudence, without which all other virtues remain stillborn. In doing so we will keep an eye, of course, on Parkinson's Laws, reminders of how readily the "best-laid plans" get prolonged. And, finally, we will want to keep ourselves disposed for the contingency of someone's high distress or for the crucial issue demanding some close study, at which time the rest of the agenda has to go on hold.

"Catching one's breath" is the final large consideration. The phrase says to us, in general, Put some padding between segments of heavy duty. If, for instance, one has a stream of conferees or clients coming in, even a quick smoke between their visits is preferable to not catching one's breath at all. (How religious superiors and other authorities, over the generations, have been able to see a stream of subjects without interval or letup is beyond my comprehension. No wonder their memories so often failed them about matters discussed.)

The day, too, has to have its time-outs and its adjournments, whether for conversation, or for some exercise, or for television (I suppose I have to say), and for general reading, especially. If one does not replenish, how will one enrich, or even interest, anyone else, to say nothing of carrying the gospel effectively to an outside world where they actually live? The old Church had its "Hours" and fixed times of prayer. The new one needs, just as much, its privileged moments – "flexible" ones maybe, but not less real. Only in such times taken out of time, really, does the hodgepodge take shape, with assistance from that most useful of all prayers, "Help!"

Finally, one has to plan ahead for the more substantial refresher. "Let's get out of here for awhile" is a strategy that we hear of even in the New Testament. To sum up, the whole self needs reviving periodically, a process that has to center on catching that breath that is God's Spirit.

Does all of this sound utopian? No doubt, but without utopias, without some positive program, no matter how much the poor thing will be infringed on, our chances for getting very far along the road diminish. The world being what it is, of course, a heavy load is likely to be one's lot a good deal of the time. So, please, somebody, keep that warm plate ready.

REFLECTION AND ACTION

Food for Thought:

Assess how Martha-like you may be. Estimate frankly the extent of your need for time-outs, the kind of channel changes that help the most, and how faithful you are in taking them.

Suggested Steps:

Think of those around you who badly need "a pause that refreshes," and help them get it.

A FEW BEATITUDES

Our Christian calling, the challenge of the gospel, is radical. It flies in the face of a whole set of values, or attitudes, much too readily accepted as normal. According to St. Matthew, Jesus made this point at the very outset of his Sermon on the Mount. The Sermon opens with a series of paradoxes, wisdom sayings, that tell us, "This will make you happy." Hence they are called "beatitudes." They concern circumstances that most people fly from. Beatitudes are contained elsewhere in Scripture, singly. This is their one concentration.

To people adept in the way of the world, this set of minority attitudes can seem pretty impractical, pretty naive, in short, utopian. Those who live by these contrastive, these idealistic attitudes are going to keep getting hurt. This, at least, is what they will be hearing in chorus from the sidelines.

"Majority Report"

1.
Poor Ray, you know,
pocket without a cent.
Every buck he garners
given out or lent.

Same old cotton shirt
begging a wash,
and the holy shoes
with their mud slosh.

Poor guy, still gassing up
the fish-tail car.
Still picks up riders.

Alive so far!

For the wife and kids
I'd wish him sense.
A poor figure, Ray.
Makes a friend wince.

2.
assert
sell your
stand up for
toot your
speak out

don't
be the last to
wallflower
gunshy
a mouse

3.
 a man's world's closed
to a holy joe

fellow gets some God
in the head and he goes off it

the born again, like drinkers,
can never get enough

too many already of the God-
hungry. it's not healthy

just between us, boy

4.
Rose now
a real problem
takes things to heart
like Ethiopia
those little rib cages
get in her talk

no sooner someone dies
Rose's there to help
must keep a pot on
for funerals

just mention
the street kids
dealing and using
the runaways
or beaten blues
presto eyes water

Not many laughs
in a day like hers

5.
Come on, Samaritan,
come on, keep moving.
You wanna stop
and be sued?

6.
a list of the plain dumb

lodger lodging a complaint
against the noisemakers

college roommate pounding
when the smile sign's locked on

a corporate whistle blower

witness witnessing against the gang

the blessed fools!

7.
In a rift of spouses
don't get your fingers jammed.

Arab will boil at Jew
to their dying day.

Get brothers into business
and you'll see bad blood.

Try breaking up a dogfight,
you get bit.

Keep your nose clean,
let them go at it.

8.
in the fairy tale
he waits and waits until she is grown up
in the fairy tale
they welcome a Downs infant
in the fairy tale
he does fine work that no one's eye will see
in the fairy tale
she gives her kidney to a relative unknown
in the fairy tale

she stays to nurse him when he's laid flat

Pearl is the best response to irritation
in the fairy tale
in the fairy tale

REFLECTION AND ACTION

This chapter may be a poser. Think about it. Where relevant, let it affect your way of acting.

CHAPTER SIX

LIVING BY FAITH

INWARDNESS

My mother's drawn in her antennae,
as age does. We have long ago told
what needed telling. Now buttering,
letting the waiter rain pepper,
she scrutinizes the tables.
We have been doing this for years.
They are an elbow away.

I fend off what I hear, so much
undressing. The Insufferable Ego,
the love net, endless explanation,
dissecting of fellow workers,
sky high hopes, fraying of what's
held. They edge into theology,
and I burst to comment.

Waiters recede. I hear, "Funny,
I've never been in church, nobody
brought me. Something seems missing."
And her companion: "I grew up there.
My father's a minister. I can't
imagine what." My mother, unaccountably,
deals one of her old sharp looks.

114

Out of the corner of these busy days, we keep seeing the youth of many a country marching off against the flower of another's. There they are, thrown at one another in anger before they can chew on troublesome questions – one of the age-old injustices of the world. A foot soldier in Shakespeare's *Henry V* puts it succinctly: "I am afeard there are few die well that die in a battle, for how can they charitably dispose of any thing, when blood is their argument?" (act 4, scene 1).

"Charitably dispose" – what could that mean? Here is one answer: acting without rancor, and without impatience for results; acting with respect for the opposite party, with that love for the neighbor that Simone Weil called "creative attention." Weil said we need "the power of God, present in us, to really think the human quality into the victims of affliction," the people left at our mercy. Warfare, in any form, seems to presuppose, on the contrary, a kind of fever; and paradoxically it ends up inducing what was called in the Vietnam era "the thousand-yard stare," a numb but calculating look. People embattled for causes often end up as their victims, consumed.

Our ideology and our idealism – a pair, if not identical, at least related – are full of such terminology as "struggle," "commitment," "solidarity." Those who are active in movements, from Birthright to Nuclear Freeze, bewail apathy and noninvolvement wherever they find it, as well they might. But rather than bewail or harangue, perhaps the movement person had much better spend energy exploring how his or her burning concern coincides with the true human quest, the quest upon which most people timidly embark and to which their talk alludes only at unguarded moments – the quest to become an individual before God. When Jesus said, "Seek first the kingdom of God and his justice," he did not mean, with simple equivalency, "So go straight out there on behalf of prisoners' rights" or "Stand up for a living wage."

He meant, "Seek that condition of your own spirit where these concerns may take root, precisely because you hold yourself attentive to God and right before God."

Kierkegaard has perhaps put the above most memorably in his "Edifying Address," one of a series that he entitled *Purity of Heart*. There is always something unsettling about Kierkegaard, but also something bracing. "In the midst of earth's appalling prodigality with human beings," as he puts it, one must not lose oneself in the mass; one is called to be responsible, to live by conscience. For Kierkegaard, conscience is not some kind of Kantian imperative or moral duty; it is more like the impulse of Abraham who sees what he must do before God.

At the high tide of Romanticism, Kierkegaard, using that term dearest to the Romantic vocabulary, "the individual," cut through all swaggering nationalism and all indulgence of the ego with his question, "My listener, do you at present live in such a way that you are yourself clearly and eternally conscious of being an individual?" He repeated this question in a variety of forms, tying it more precisely to the domestic life, to the fostering of a career, and to civic action.

> Even in these relations which we so beautifully style the most intimate of all, do you remember that you have a still more intimate relation, namely, that in which you as an individual are related to yourself before God? . . . Are you of one mind about the manner in which you will carry out your occupation, or is your mind continually divided because you wish to be in harmony with the crowd? . . . If you live in a populous city, and you direct your attention outwards, sympathetically engrossing yourself in the people and in what is going on, do you remember each time you throw yourself in this way into the world around you, that in this relation you relate yourself to yourself as an individual with eternal responsibility?

In everything that he wrote, this prophetic and evangelical man sought for true inwardness. He was continually disturbed and puzzled that so few seemed to value this condition, or that so many let themselves be pushed away from it. How few, as he put it, are alert to the Absolute Paradox, that consequence of the incarnation whereby the Eternal is in one place and at one time to be met by the lone individual, who can respond – despite sinfulness – actively, dynamically, in "the rising passion of faith" (Perry D. LeFevre, *The Prayers of Kierkegaard*).

If Kierkegaard was, par excellence, "That Individual," Simone Weil was the truth seeker. Weil, a French Jew, found herself born "inside the faith" and described herself as one living "at the intersection of Christianity and everything that is not Christianity." In the turbulence of the 1930s and 1940s she intently sought purity of heart. Her letter "Spiritual Autobiography" to Father Perrin, which is included in *Waiting for God*, tells the story movingly. She, a child of privilege who took on the slavery of factory work, a peace lover who had joined the Loyalist forces in Spain, could point out, toward the end of her short life, that "social enthusiasms, which have such power today and raise people so effectively to the supreme degree of heroism in suffering and death," are something "essentially different" from the love of Christ. This love can permeate them, but not necessarily. The real test will come, she points out, when those who are "momentarily least strong" come to prevail over some oppression. How then will they act? Will some inwardness express itself, or will the determinant be raw power and the forcing of means to ends?

The poet Adrienne Rich, in her poem "A Vision," which addresses itself to Simone Weil, has cried out in protest at the austere toils and self-deprivation that Weil practiced; she decries above all the fixity of Weil's gaze upon the Burning One, God. But Rich is wrong to explain as a psychological warp, or to take as a betrayal of Feminism, what ran much deeper in Simone Weil, a woman who was wary even of the normal procedures of prayer. If purity of heart, as Kierkegaard says, is to will the one thing, "the one necessary thing," she was willful; yet hers was the opposite of self-concern. And the moments of grace that followed from such striving were a sheer surprise. For instance, during the recitation of George Herbert's poem "Love," she says, "Christ himself came down and took possession of me." While she was studying the Our Father, "the infinite sweetness of the Greek text so took hold of me that for several days I could not stop myself from saying it over all the time." The Our Father continued to have this effect: "Though I experience it each day, it exceeds my expectation at each repetition."

Perhaps a vocation to prayer is the truest thing that both Kierkegaard and Simone Weil display. They enacted it in unique ways, but their life stories make it clear that the call to prayer is not a generic invitation to spend time on one's knees or do some detached meditating. It means coming to recognize, before God, the truths about oneself: one's specific gifts, which only become clear after a time; one's generous and persistent dreams; the faults one bares to the Lord for forgiveness; the edge of craziness that persists, often lifelong; the identity to which grace slowly forms a person.

In our present era, the restaurant, the place of dining in public, is where people seem to talk most intimately, to reveal themselves even without intending to do so. One who listens, who perhaps cannot help but overhear, will occasionally catch the note, the appeal, the longing for this inwardness without which we are not yet truly individuals in the sense of Kierkegaard, that is, before God.

REFLECTION AND ACTION

Food for Thought:

Reread the part of this chapter that has to do with Kierkegaard, aiming to understand, from his standpoint, the concept of "inwardness" and the designation of him as "That Individual."

Suggested Steps:

St. Luke has a way of reminding us that Jesus kept slipping away for some prayer – Jesus the busiest of people. In your most demanding occupation, try doing that – but remind yourself that the physical getaway or the chapel time is not what's essential.

I WILL BE TRUE TO YOU

1.
"I will be true right to
the finish line." "You?"

"You have my word." "Words!
So many fizzled children."

"We'll shake. Put 'er there,
firm." "Firm, that grip?!"

"Bring me a paper then, I'll sign."
"You sign and the moon shines."

"I beg you, invest in me."
"Bank simply upon you?"

"If not, poof goes my trust."
"Trust more than your own air."

2.
Please, make my yes mean yes.

Not a day fails
its promise of sunrise.

I'm thumbing the register
of providential dealings.
The book's immense.
At the last chapter
promise is made flesh.

Root me in you, promise,
flower from me.

In my gloomier moments, I get to wondering how anyone can emit a promise, even one limited in scope, even one having to do with payment and service. What daring that seems to call for. As to making the long-term commitment – the solemn sort called vows – only babes in the woods would do that, my good sense tells me.

When I promise even something small, I know the difficulty of keeping up to the mark. I have been at planning sessions or committee meetings where we all agreed to do something before the next meeting, and in my heart of hearts have known how unlikely I was to follow through. Although socialized to stability, and predisposed to it, I am conscious of leaning on a frail reed when I promise.

What about the young who grow up today with a cornucopia of possibilities – the channel surfers and interactive shoppers? The modern person is one who insists on keeping the options open. Speak not to such a one of promises. When you promise something you choose one direction and close off others. In the atmosphere of "openness," the concept of "promise" seems pretty ominous.

When I taught in college and lived in the student dorms, resident assistants and others had outings and projects to organize. I noticed what would happen to their "best-laid plans" because it often happened to mine; lots of initial enthusiasm and many sign-ups, but when it came to the actual date, when students had to deliver on their pledge, only about 50 percent would do so. The organizers, especially for retreats and trips, would say, "All right, we'll make them pay such and such, so they will feel themselves involved." But this merely pushed the signees to buy their way out of commitments ("OK, so I lose $10 or $20").

Weddings are the most frequent public instances of a promise. With what eagerness and hopefulness most young people take on the immense task of lifelong companionship and collaboration. And what a short distance they can see ahead. How little they recognize of even their own problematic side, their deficiencies likely to cause trouble.

"Oh! Youth!" exclaims the narrator of the Joseph Conrad story "Youth: A Narrative," recalling the thrill of his first nautical command. He had to get a coal scow from England to Indonesia before the cargo all combusted spontaneously. He lost the battle in sight of port, yet somehow the struggle itself exhilarated him. "Oh, the glamour of youth! Oh, the fire of it," says the narrator, an older man shaking his more sober head in humorous wonder. How do we dare take on such impossible things?

Today the bets are against any given marital union going the distance. This is immensely sad. The reasons are everywhere to seek, though this is not the place to do so. A starry-eyed approach to the altar, reliance on one's own integrity and follow-through, on one's own energy and decency and native kindness come woefully short of the task at hand. The most peerless-looking couples are often the first to separate.

The context of sacrament is truly crucial for those pledging their love, even though the blessing can hardly conjure away the deficiencies each person brings. Matrimony is a sacrament precisely as a source of grace – the Lord's support and strength tendered daily to a couple striving, against obstacles, to give witness to the power of lasting love.

I have to chuckle, recognizing how many of us pledged ourselves to God in religious life forty or so years ago at age nineteen. "O! Youth!" How could we presume? Many later came to the judgment, often enough correct, that they shouldn't have. As for ourselves, how grateful we are for what was once called the grace of perseverance – which is to say, the Lord's daily support. At age nineteen, how much bewilderment, how many developmental crises, how many challenges to courage and to initiative and to what Bernard Lonergan called an "appropriation" of the vowed life lay ahead. In our prayer, how much crying out to the Lord there would have to be, and how many "Fear not" assurances in response. As for our former companions, how many of them, ideals still high, kept the deepest and most basic commitment, that to holy faith: "We will be true to thee till death."

Rabbi Harold Kushner, in *Who Needs God*, quotes William James in *The Varieties of Religious Experience*, his classic, as dividing religious people into the "once-born" and the "twice-born." As Kushner explains, "The once-born are people who sail through life without ever experiencing anything that shatters or complicates their faith." They may have financial reverses, problems with their children, and so forth, but they always feel that a kindly God is controlling things. James's twice-born souls, on the other hand, are people who lose their faith and then regain a very different one. They come out with "a less cheerful, less confident, more realistic outlook. God is no longer the parent who keeps them safe and dry. He is the power that enables them to keep going in a stormy and dangerous world." John Henry Newman, in his *Parochial and Plain Sermons,* chimed in on this subject under the provocative title "Promising Without Doing." Said Newman, "Our religious professions are at a far greater distance from our acting upon them than we ourselves are aware." Our naive assessment comes from our "mistaking good feelings for real religious principle." We are not properly conscious, he says, of the burden that hangs upon our will and tends to clog it.

Newman, in those pre-Catholic days, even spoke of "our corrupt nature." This may be an excessive concept, especially as applied to the baptized, but how astute Newman's observation: "We can never answer how we shall act under new circumstances. A very little knowledge of life and of our own hearts will teach us this." So what shall we do? Venture nothing? Bury away our talent? No indeed. But in our promising, we must depend constantly on the One who, as Newman puts it, "knoweth whereof we are made and alone can uphold us. . . . There can be no harm in professing much directly to God, because, while we speak, we know He sees through our professions, and takes them for what they really are, prayers."

"Help me be faithful" is what we say when promising before God. For the once-born that prayer takes on a certain perky tonality. The twice-born, saying the same thing, are holding on for dear life. Fifty years ago, perhaps, certain benign arrangements favored the once-born. The world works against them now in every way. This should not freeze up the capacity for promising, which is still precious, still at the heart of being human. As to those who once promised generously and now, still on the trail, look back from far along, marveling and exclaiming "O! Youth!" like Conrad's narrator, what words can fit their tempered awareness? A verse of the psalms, perhaps: "Not to us, O Lord, not to us, but to your name give glory" (Ps. 115).

REFLECTION AND ACTION

Food for Thought:
　　Even while remembering Marianne Moore's observation that the mind is "not a Herod's oath that cannot change" (from "The Mind Is an Enchanting Thing"), and that promises differ widely in gravity, give some thought to how lightly or seriously you make your own.

Suggested Steps:
　　In the spirit of Newman, turn your promising into praying.

THE COURAGE TO BE

　　　to heave yourself out of bed
　　　into the day's scowl,

　　　step into the rider's seat
　　　when you find the door dented,

　　　keep from shaving truth
　　　with the blade of diplomacy;

　　　to pick up the nagging receiver,
　　　or just plain own up;

　　　set the memo aside when hot
　　　and let it cool,

　　　raise questions
　　　with one who controls by anger;

to let your little ones
out of the tight circle,

dwell in the family of pain
and not take it ill.

Growing up, I did a lot of hiking with my father. Our favorite topic as we walked was the baseball legends of his youth in Washington, D.C., especially the pitcher Walter Johnson. I liked to play baseball but was only passable at it, which I will blame partly on ground balls. You have to get down to field the ground ball. "Keep your eye on it," coaches would shout. But I shied from the hot ones, given their penchant for a nasty hop. Guns were another thing that, as a city boy, I shied from. Our Jesuit high school had R.O.T.C., but on the strength of a few clarinet lessons, I got myself into the R.O.T.C. band. World War II was happening to my elders, the Korean War would happen soon to my contemporaries, and I had little stomach for bullets whizzing around. In Stephen Crane's novel *The Red Badge of Courage,* a staple of high-school reading, I had no trouble imagining the flight of young recruits from the battlefield.

To put it briefly, the topic of courage has long been at the back of my mind. Nerve, energy against obstacles, readiness for conflict – that comes more readily to some than to others, as Aristotle pointed out in his *Ethics.* It is strongest in the young, which makes them very liable to drafting. Perhaps those who have less of this wonderful force are more aware of it. With me it always took some special mustering.

With adulthood, the context modifies. For women, including adolescent women, childbearing has to pose a great test of courage. Never mind that almost all women must pass that way, the next one in line is still tried mightily. With childrearing, the demands soften, it would seem, but how unremitting they become. Demands complexify and accumulate for everyone as life goes on. Courage can amount to facing just one solitary day, the one that is waiting to take a hundred bites. Emily Dickinson, as we might expect, put the matter succinctly:

> To fight aloud, is very brave –
> But *gallanter*, I know
> Who charge within the bosom
> The cavalry of Woe. (#126)

Marianne Moore extended the domain of courage into the realm of the big questions about life and death. In her poem "What Are Years?" she asks,

> And whence
> is courage: the unanswered question,
> the resolute doubt, –
> dumbly calling, deafly listening – that
> in misfortune, even death,
> encourages others
> and in its defeat, stirs
> the soul to be strong?

Paul Tillich, the philosophic theologian, strikes a chord merely with the title of his book, *The Courage to Be*. Wilhelm Pauck, in *The Thought of Paul Tillich* (ed. James L. Adams, Pauck and Roger L. Shinn), writes: "For Tillich life was filled with anxiety resulting from the threat of nonbeing that inheres in finiteness, an anxiety that appears in three forms: that of fate and death, that of emptiness and meaninglessness and that of guilt and condemnation" (42). Ann Belford Ulanov, in this same volume, pursues the topic. "In his willingness to combat the anxiety of nonbeing, Paul Tillich received and welcomed anything that promised to enlarge his – and others' – courage to be" (119).

According to Tillich, says Ulanov, "we are anxious that we will be swept away, lost in currents of undifferentiated emotions, needs, and drives, never to be able again to form ourselves into a discrete entity, to become a person who can hold it all. . . . We refuse to admit into awareness all the bits of being available to us – in our emotions, images, ambitions, needs, hurts, longings – and so they remain there in the shadows, undeveloped and unrealized" (18). Also "an abundance of meanings . . . confounds us" (130). "We flee into a defense of our small and partial view," when in fact life is addressing us in some fragment of experience, confronting us, handing us something of great importance. According to Tillich, love alone is the responsive opening that allows us to be ourselves.

Even in the most savage conditions, as Tillich and other survivors of the Nazis such as Viktor Frankl point out, Being summons us. If this sounds like existentialist philosophy, in a way it is; but Tillich was always also the Lutheran pastor, reminding us what trouble we have facing the presence of God, the "presence that can turn a disastrous blow into a source of renewal, a grace that points to the fact of goodness dwelling there, real, alive, in the midst of terrible evil" (132). A positive response takes faith.

A generation ago many of us Jesuits were convoked for a community-building weekend that included the exercise of picking and sharing a favorite passage from the New Testament, one holding a high charge of personal meaning. I remember in our small group of eight that three people, including myself, picked the episode of the storm on the lake. According to Matthew, Mark, and Luke, Jesus is awakened by panicky apostles from his sleep at the stern of the boat, and chides them, "Why are you afraid, you weak believers?" In John 6 he comes walking over the turbulent water with the same message. Our Lord's sure approach over the roiled waters is still the gist of the Good News. Does the world seem to be convulsing under our feet? God seeks us out. God is with us. Only have faith.

REFLECTION AND ACTION

Food for Thought:
    With adult frankness, take a reading on your own meas-
ure and quality of courage. Every life, remember, bears a
large unnoticed quotient of courage. Note also that our
courage is bound to be finite; this is why we pray in the Our
Father, "bring us not to the test."

Suggested Steps:
    If there is something waiting out there for you to do,
but you just have not dared, now might be a good time.

AFTER THE LAST CLASS

    I'm behind the rounded shoulders of Our Lord
    and the bold letters "Learn from me."
    How still. What a moon hangs there
    with its continents, between a palm tree
    and a thinning olive from old Mission days.
    Chairs have unfolded on the lawn
    by thousands, attentive for the brass notes
    of commencement. Under a long canopy
    the watchman whiles. I have this day read
    "La Dernière Classe," and taught it.
    ("Never desert the language you are born to.")
    Everything – planes flitting in
    like fireflies, the top of Swig Hall dorm,
    the adobe wall – says "Learn of me."
    I am a small part of the picture. Who's
    that? The young approaching behind me.

Twenty years ago, almost to this day, I was teaching the prose
of Matthew Arnold and John Henry Newman. I had just
begun my long stretch in the classroom at Santa Clara
University. It was a boiling time on the college campus

because American troops had just entered Cambodia and students at Kent State had been killed while expressing outrage. At Santa Clara there was a big protest rally, which I remember attending with some uneasiness. A delegation went from our school to join a mass protest in Washington, D.C. What reminds me of that just now is a slip of paper I find in my *Norton Anthology*: "The men who went to D.C. went as delegates of S.C.U. They had no right to do so." I seem to have feared they would be taken as emissaries of our president and faculty!

Professors and students on our campus in the spring of 1970 organized a boycott of classes. I, however, failing to see a connection between fury against the U.S. government and the cessation of classes, persisted in discoursing on Arnold and Newman. About half the students came. (A day or so later the school year was terminated abruptly.) I now look back with a shock of recognition on the underlinings in our text for that fateful class. From Matthew Arnold we studied "The Function of Criticism at the Present Time." Arnold, a late Victorian, from an age harping insistently on fixed ideas, pleads for "the free play of the mind" on two sides of a question, and for what he calls "disinterestedness" in approaching even the most politically sensitive issues. Wanting us "to see things as they are," he speaks even about embracing, despite all the pressures of practicality, "the Indian virtue of detachment." Imagine, detachment at the moment of a military invasion!

Arnold's horizon was defined by the spires of his alma mater, Oxford. So was that of John Henry Newman. The excerpts from Newman that we pondered back in 1970 took liberal education itself as their subject. We may call an education liberal, Newman claims, when it produces not so much techniques and solutions as a "philosophical temper," a "general culture of the mind," an enlargement and comprehensiveness of outlook. Knowledge in a university setting, Newman declared, is not a matter of "direct and simple vision"; it proceeds, rather, "by piecemeal and accumulation, by a mental process, by going round an object, by the comparison, the combination, the mutual correction, the continual adaptation of many partial notions." In this pithy account of a gradual truth-seeking method, we have the seed of what later flowered as *A Grammar of Assent* – Newman's attempt to trace the interaction between reason and faith in the case of an ordinary believer. Newman's mode of inductive reasoning appealed to me so mightily as a way through the welter of contemporary ideas that when a national emergency arose, I think I resented it and fought it off as an incursion.

Derek Bok, the president of Harvard, recently singled out Newman as spokesman for the university "as a place detached from society, uncontaminated by its worldly values." From our present viewpoint – amid national and ethnic uprisings, gay-power initiatives, the battle against the international AIDS plague, and the mobilization of women in politics, ethics, and ecclesiology – Newman's image of the intellectual may suggest a hapless figure: the pipe-smoking academic always ready to consider things from yet another angle ("Now, class, for the theory of so-and-so") but never ready to settle on a position of his own. And truly, if there is a vice proper to the campus (besides that of jockeying for promotion), is it not the vice of playing with ideas instead of staking one's life on them? But John Henry Newman was one who had staked his life; he was no patron of the ivory tower.

John Henry Newman, in his June 1852 lectures on *The Scope and Nature of University Education*, was not just daydreaming. He was proposing a blueprint for an actual Catholic university, which the Irish bishops had just asked him to establish in Dublin. The bishops felt themselves pushed into the project; they had little enthusiasm for it. Meriol Trevor, Newman's biographer, says:

> It is clear that even Cullen [archbishop of Dublin], the only Irish bishop who had supported the idea of a Catholic university (because Roman policy was against "mixed" education [i.e., with Protestants]) really expected nothing more than a college, a kind of lay seminary, controlled by priests. . . . Newman shocked him by the freedom he allowed the students and the laymen [including nationalistic Young Irelanders] he appointed to the staff.

> And then Newman's educational aims seemed startlingly modern – scientific faculties and a school of medicine (which flourished more than any). . . . What was more, Newman gave lectures to the faculties assuring them a proper intellectual freedom, just as he allowed the students a proper moral freedom. . . . He was not a commander or director; he treated others as equals, as being capable of a responsibility they did not always show. In an era strong in father figures, Newman preferred brotherhood.

In a strong hierarchical and dogmatic era of the Church, Newman, the probing convert, aroused much suspicion. Partisan spirits did not take kindly to his perspective. So he found himself almost alone in a task that preoccupied him: to engage and respond to the secular spirit. Here are the goals Newman aimed at in his *University* lectures: to help Catholics read with some sympathy and insight the mostly Protestant literature in English; to assure students of science that evolutionary findings would not destroy the faith; and to encourage honest biblical study. He insisted that theology must be the integrating subject, central to the life of the mind. If Derek Bok and others find that Newman leaned toward contemplative composure, it was for the purpose of theology – that is, to study the implications of revealed truth. Theology does not stand alone, Newman said, but in relationship to many partial views of human and material reality.

To the "victims of an intense self-contemplation," it reveals the transcendent, "the whole truth" (discourses 4 and 8). Today, after twenty years of university teaching, rereading Newman on the centenary of his death, I am awed by his penetration and his prescience. He seemed to be responding, in the mid-nineteenth century, to our university climate today, as described by Robert Kiely in the "Religion and Education" issue of *Daedalus* (Spring 1988):

> One impression that is commonly given to American undergraduates when they first arrive on a university campus is that truly educated and smart people cannot continue to be believers. Of course, there are chaplaincies and comparative religion courses and, in some universities, excellent divinity schools, but the primary message is that religion is private, peripheral, and intellectually suspect. For thousands of students, this message must seem like part of an Alice-in-Wonderland reversal, since in the world in which they have grown up religion is public and central.

Since Newman's time, the challenges of secularity have not paled but have intensified. Post-Kantian skepticism about the adequacy of language to establish any contact with the real predominates. Metaphysics has been relegated to the status of science fiction. In the not-so-old days, a Jesuit college graduate went forth secure (naively, of course) in the belief that "the perennial philosophy" was a key to unlock any door. How much more frequent now, and almost unavoidable, is relativistic thinking – or hard-line thinking, by reaction.

The temper of mind that Newman called for as normal in the university turns out now to be pretty rare. At Santa Clara recently we had a pro-choice versus pro-life debate – definitely a first. What would Newman think of such an event? Impossible to say, of course. But he did lay down the principle, in his *University* lectures, that "Truth is bold and unsuspicious," and he asked, in consequence, Why keep opponents from speaking "if you think that your friends have reason on their side as fully as your opponents" (discourse 4)? But he would no doubt be aghast at the media tactics of our time, at the amplified pitch and volume and consequent distortions more proper to a rally than to a serious conversation.

I am at this juncture of my life leaving the classroom, switching away from the strenuous task of correcting and recorrecting papers but also from the continual stimulus that a university provides. (Religious journalism may in fact provide me more of the same.) Looking back on these twenty years in the classroom, I can see how the ideas of Newman were doing their quiet work on me. As a teacher of literature – of the books and writers, mostly, that I had wanted the opportunity to study – I have gone with students in and out of worlds that clash with my own deepest values, that are ecstatic, or depressed, or exotic, or skeptical, or even sinister, in ways foreign to my own sensibility.

Often in class I was able to return to Dante and T. S. Eliot, to Langston Hughes and Marianne Moore, and to other writers I found sympathetic. But much more important than the paydirt of favorite authors was the opportunity to range over the field with my students, weighing values along with them and laboring to clarify our human understanding and our commitments. Take as an example of an unforgettable but problematic text the villanelle of Dylan Thomas, "Do Not Go Gentle into That Good Night." Thomas, modulating high- and low-frequency vowels with perfect command, subtly managing the overtones of words, sings the reader and the hearer into a certain attitude – that is, into a stance of bitter resistance before death. Pity that this approach to dying is one that I cannot accept because it seems at odds with the Christian attitude. I only wish that I had capitalized better on this discrepancy so as to debate it more fully with my students.

It dawns on me now, even as I write, that the very language of Newman's lectures, such as "Christianity and Letters," and of his poignant *Apologia pro Vita Sua,* and of his orations when Catholicism was legitimized in England (*The Present Position of Catholics in England*) became pervasive in my own language. As a writer and a teacher of composition, after I had imbibed Newman I had to unlearn his Ciceronian, or periodic, way of speaking, with its careful balance of related elements. After all, the clipped sentence full of active verbs is the idiom of our times. (See chapter 4, "Wisewriting," which admits allegiance to that more spicy mode.) It is what readers today enjoy and expect. Still, I think I never did unlearn Newman. Perhaps this influence of his explains the trouble I had accomplishing in class what students most of all expect, "making one thing perfectly clear."

According to Professor David De Laura (lecture at Santa Clara University, May 4, 1989), the voice of Newman actually haunted the nineteenth century. Matthew Arnold called it "the most entrancing of voices, subtle, sweet, mournful." Others judged it "clear, intense, piercing," or found "a severe, tender voice, a simple but studied delivery." Newman knew what he was about, "the power of the transcendent located in the voice," as De Laura puts it. To Newman, who entitled one of his talks "Personal Influence as the Means of Promoting the Truth," the truth conveyer is not a disembodied medium but a person. The witness is a subject. In the years after Vatican Council II this notion has become familiar. John Henry Newman with his Oxford ethos, fitting uneasily into his Catholic milieu, turns up as a sympathetic spirit in our milieu – certainly in mine.

My poem "After the Last Class" came as I was preparing a brief tribute to Newman as part of the concluding prayer at our graduation ceremony. I wandered out of Nobili Hall, Santa Clara University, about 9:00 p.m. after a long day, and there in the Mission Gardens, from my standpoint near a statue of the Sacred Heart, was the scene. Much earlier that day my mind had wandered elsewhere, to when I was a seminary student first learning French. We were taught vocabulary and structure through the short stories of Alphonse Daudet, especially "La Dernière Classe," set in the 1870s. So I had gone and looked up Daudet again.

In "La Dernière Classe" a man who has taught French grammar to Alsatian children for forty years learns from the invading Prussians that there is to be "no more French." He gives his pupils a sad and simple farewell: "Do not forget the language that you were born into." John Henry Newman is a language I was born into. On this centenary year of his death at the Birmingham Oratory on August 11, 1890, I want to remember.

REFLECTION AND ACTION

Food for Thought:

Free play of the mind, disinterestedness, detachment, the philosophical temper – reflect on how practical or achievable you may find this condition to be.

Suggested Steps:

Let this be the place for some extended recognition and gratitude toward those who have most influenced your thinking.

CHAPTER SEVEN

DEVOTION

RIGHT SPIRIT

Lord, Spirit of Jesus,
aid us along his path
to toddle, walk,
    and run.

Clasp of the Son and Father,
draw into accord
the races, sexes,
    nations.

Wide open secret,
spread the gospel truth
to homes, offices,
    assemblies.

Voice in the judge's ear,
enter a plea for us
by his birth, toils,
    and life blood.

Sisterly guide,
help us dwell in God
by our opinions, words,
    and choices.

Promise of Jesus,
shape us to a body
by his gifts and cross
and love.*

I write this on a weekend in San Francisco, very brisk. The wind blowing off the ocean swells out the sails in the bay. How exhilarating to walk across the city today! Your breathing is done for you. After months in a large smog belt far out of state, the time is just right for the return of the native.

I think I perceive something today about the notion of spirit, how it fills us out, sweeps into us, as it were, and catches us up, as happened to the first timid disciples. Something in us responds to a force coming upon us. Consider the scene of Pentecost: wind, flame, tongues; an unseen force, burning excitement, utterance. The listless followers are brought to life from within.

Without this infusion of energy, says the Psalm (104), every creature droops and begins to shrivel. With it we feel ourselves buoyed up, even against immense obstacles. Our love, up to then flagging, by no means engaging all of our heart, soul, strength, and mind, gets a new impetus. So we have a daily need, as humans and believers, to pray, "Come, Holy Spirit." It is a prayer of equal standing with the one we address to "our Father" – "Your kingdom come" – and with the outburst of longing at the end of the New Testament: "Come, Lord Jesus." For the Spirit is our entree into the life of God; from the Spirit derives our thirst for the divine; it is, finally, the Spirit who faces us toward Jesus, "the holy one of God" (Mk. 1:24).

---

* This poem has been set to music (in four parts) by Kevin Garvin under the title "The Spirit's Song."

Jesus transmits to us, according to the Gospel of John, a message that we find almost impossible to register: It is better for me to be physically gone, out of reach, than to stay here in your midst, for then my Spirit can come to dwell. Jesus inculcates a transition from the without to the within. We need to pass from external accompaniment and observation of him, where we maintain our own standpoint, to interior union and full sharing of outlook. Jesus, after his resurrection, made this new interior condition possible, entering not just into the supper room but into the inner life of his followers.

According to Paul, "By his resurrection from the dead Jesus was designated Son of God in power according to the Spirit of holiness" (Rom 1:4). He was permeated by the Spirit bodily, so that Paul could say elsewhere, "The Lord is Spirit" (2 Cor 3:17, 18) and therefore able to send the Spirit forth as his very own, to those who are his own. When we say "Holy Spirit," in other words, we mean "Spirit of Jesus," the One who moves us according to the mind or attitude of Christ, and penetrates us with it. David M. Coffey explains this theological reality:

> Christ is the content of the Gift of the Holy Spirit, who is the Spirit of Christ; and where Christ is, there too is the Father, for Christ is the sacrament of the Father, the Word of the Father. . . . The content of the first Christians' experience of the Spirit was Christ himself, because the Spirit was his love for them, [permeating and shaping his] word addressed to them, the gospel, and thus bringing Him to them. ("A Proper Mission of the Holy Spirit," *Theological Studies*, June 1986, 238-39.)

The first impression that we get from that fiery presence at Pentecost is of a common spirit, a unifying and shared force, not a private gift to a particular holy person nor anyone's monopoly. The coming of the Spirit is formative of the church; a living and breathing family within God is created from this timorous handful of individuals. St. Paul put it with his usual directness: "God did not give us a spirit of fearfulness but one of power and of love and of clear judgment" (2 Tim 1:7). The last of these terms indicates that Paul, respecting as he had to the unpredictable gifts of the Holy Spirit, saw also, from the start, the need to test them and the priority in Christian life of the right choice.

It is important to reiterate what should be quite obvious, that no one has a monopoly on spirit. This Spirit of God that "moved over the waters," and "contains everything," and "has covered all the globe," is not to be confined to the explicit membership of one assembly. Even as it labors to form the body of Christ out of reluctant materials, it works with people groping toward God sometimes from a far remove. God takes us where we are. After all, "our forefathers upon this continent" were touched by a strong sense of God as Great Spirit, long before the beaching of the Mayflower with the first Christians. In our own times the Spirit speaks still through unexpected voices – artists and movements and forms of thought not patently theistic. Often the voice emerges only after we spend some time sorting things out; all the more important not to miss it.

Nonetheless, in the Christian understanding, the Holy Spirit does have as final aim nothing more nor less than the upbuilding of Christ. To this end has the church been enriched by its gifts and fruits. Among these are distinct spiritualities widely familiar in the Catholic family – frameworks for the Christian life according to St. Francis, St. Basil, St. Ignatius, St. Theresa, St. Vincent de Paul, or some religious pioneer of our own century, such as Charles de Foucauld, Dorothy Day, Mother Theresa, Father Cardijn (of the Young Christian Workers and the Christian Family Movement), Jean Vanier (of l'Arche). These "diverse showings of the spirit" (1 Cor 12:5), these particular Christian emphases translated into daily life, have helped individuals answer a given calling or exploit a talent – a contemplative bent, an affection for the poor, a hunger for the truth, an urge to be of service.

Spiritualities of a defined type, it must be admitted, run the danger of hardening, of turning parochial. The working of the Holy Spirit is more pervasive, wide-ranging, unitive, and subtle and discriminating than any specific form of life, and is the test of them all. "Spirituality," over and beyond its patterns or forms, has always implied an experiencing subject and thus an individualizing of religion. What we allude to by the term is, above all, a certain focus on the inner life, some mode of attentiveness to the divine, a habit of prayer including self-examination and awareness of God's action. We try in our quest, our pilgrim's way, to avoid the counterfeit – anemic or distorted forms that leave out, or perhaps disdain, what is of the body, such as expressions and even dramas of affection, such as exercise and athletics and hard labor, or that legitimize a kind of discouragement about the world, a disinterest in the daily news, a nonengagement in the struggle for better human conditions.

To think helpfully or with accuracy about our specific call to what is known as "the spiritual life" (which the Gospel of John refers to merely as "the life"), we begin by rejecting any disembodied notions of "spirit," and we have recourse immediately to the person who, between Father and Son, is known as Holy Spirit, or The Love. This Holy One helps us enter the life of God by undeceiving us, by bringing to the light what Jesus meant, by strengthening us to walk in the narrow way, the road of Jesus to Jerusalem, along with many fellows.

How does the Spirit act within those who are its "anointed," those marked with chrism at baptism and gifted with faith in Christ, who himself is, literally, the one "anointed" by God's Spirit? The Spirit guides us almost instinctively at some times, for example, as we react to a situation in which we find something fishy – values that seem shallow or hurtful – or as we respond to one where, on the contrary, we find enormous opportunity for good. Sometimes this happens by rebound. We come to realize, after we have passed through a difficult moment, Ah, that's what Jesus meant when saying, "Do not be anxious for yourself" or "Blessed are the meek" or "If your right eye causes you to sin, pluck it out." In other words, the Spirit of Jesus makes possible the reading of the gospel in terms of our specific lives, where Christ lives and moves.

John's Gospel speaks of the Spirit as "counselor," like an attorney giving wise advice to a long-time client and addressing the court in his or her advocacy role. St. Paul, who clearly established the equal footing of the Spirit within a holy Trinity, said, "The Spirit helps us in our weakness; for we do not know how to pray as we ought," we scarcely know what is good for us. "But the Spirit intercedes for us with sighs deeper than words" (Rom. 8:26) when, as God's sons or daughters, we want to know, for instance, What shall I do with my life? or What does God want of me? At any unsure time – when faced by crucial alternatives; with minds clouded by resentment, ambition, or fear; or when the suffering of someone we love seems too great for us to bear – we can commend ourselves, with assurance, to those "sighs deeper than words."

The Holy Spirit of God wishes to be our underlying force, a power in our lives. The famous "freedom of the Spirit" is an experience of being empowered, at liberty, to voice insights and desires, to chime in with others in their petitions and testimonies, to speak openly to the Lord. It can also be manifest in a profound sense of ingathering and quietness before God. It above all should confer a certain lightness, a sense not of obligation but of opportunity in the course of doing good.

The Holy Spirit is invoked often in a climate of tremendous psychic forces, forces with which it can and does work but with which it is not identical. These forces, of course, can be unleashed by certain techniques and manipulated, in which case freedom vanishes. So a testing of the Spirit for maturity and balance, for Christian self-possession, for what Ignatius of Loyola called "thinking with the Church," is a helpful accompaniment of the charismatic phenomena, those touches of the Spirit that have enlivened so many believers.

The Holy Spirit, in the experience of the church, is the one who keeps coming to communicate breath, meaning, hopefulness, generosity, and guidance to the body of believers as it did to the body of Christ. Spirit – hidden impetus, one's very life breath. Creator Spirit – a force of imagination, the One who can bring out potential, put things, including words, in undreamed-of order, help us find a way. As a personal presence, the Lord's Spirit waits close at hand. Upon hearing the disheartened question, "Shall these bones live?" the Holy One responds, "I'll say!"

REFLECTION AND ACTION

Food for Thought:

Our contemporaries pursue spirituality with some enthusiasm, but the concept "spirituality," and the reality aimed at, remains pretty wide open. The previous pages are an attempt ("essay") to trace the role of the Holy Spirit in conforming us to Jesus Christ. Indicate how this heavily Pauline teaching may or may not be shaping your spirituality.

Presumably the Spirit of Jesus, as counselor, is active in your life. Stop and trace how this may be happening.

Suggested Steps:

St. Ignatius Loyola, in the *Spiritual Exercises*, proposes rules for a "discernment," or testing, of the spirits, that is to say, of our interior influences. If unaware of these observations and rules, familiarize yourself with them; if aware, examine how or whether you put them into practice.

Get used to quick equivalents, or to expansions, of the prayer "Come, Holy Spirit."

MARY: DYNAMO OR FAITHFUL DISCIPLE?

Mary, how great our joy in you,
In whom the world's salvation grew;
From you he came to heal and teach,
To you his grace and favor reach.

The angel brought you God's own word,
"Yes," you replied to what you heard.
The Holy Spirit filled your room,
God took our shape within your womb.

You knew the hour of grief and loss,
The way of Jesus to the cross.
You saw your son for sinners bleed,
Mary, your faith was strong indeed.

In you our flesh has gone to God,
Whose mercies all on earth applaud.
The Church invokes its dearest one,
a portent shines like morning sun.

Sister, we prize you as our own,
Wife, you and Joseph bless the home,
Woman, we praise your warmth of heart,
Mother, we pray you, take our part.

Note: The above hymn was written to be sung to the melody of the Old Hundredth ("O God, from whom all blessings flow").

Friends and foes alike of Catholic Christianity have long identified the Blessed Virgin Mary with the Catholic Church. Is this a prejudice, a pious exaggeration, a plain fact, or what? A friend of mine some years ago, traveling in Italy, heard a Sunday sermon on the two great commandments. They turned out to be love of God and love of the Blessed Mother. The mistake is hair-raising, of course, but one can understand how the preacher got to thinking that way.

The close connection between the Virgin Mary and the Catholic Church strikes every eye. A Marian shrine has arisen five miles from where I pen these lines. A thirty-foot statue, ingeniously jointed from stainless-steel strips, shows a young-adult Mary with hands outspread as a conveyer of grace toward the motorists on Highway 101 nearby. A grassy knoll leads up to the statue, which is floodlit at night. People continually gather in curious interest, in awe, and in prayer about the statue. It arose at an enormous cost, thanks to the trusting zeal of the pastor, the encouragement and contributions of thousands, and the generosity of local contractors. It will draw great numbers of pilgrims and tourists, as the pastor points out, from the whole area between Portland and Mexico City, sites of the two nearest shrines.

Many Catholics are reassured even thrilled by the foregoing. Once on the spot it is hard not to be. Yet Marian shrines, their devotional aura, the literature available there, cause uneasiness to some who are preoccupied with the social impact of the gospel. What is the connection, they instinctively ask, between the Synod of Rome, declaring in 1971 that the pursuit of justice is a constituent of true faith, or between our present concern for the empowerment of the poor and disadvantaged, and the Virgin towering here in protection over the helpless believer? Does she not keep the believer in a kind of holy childhood or otherworldliness unworthy of adult Christians?

The medieval Mother of Mercies, with mantle outspread over bishops, priests, peasants, and housewives half her size, may find less resonance today, when individuals feel overwhelmed already and diminished by massive forces. Still, such misgivings can be calmed a bit when one recognizes, in the backward look that we call history, what enormous energy devotion to Mary has produced for changing the world. How many medieval works of charity took place under her patronage. How many hospital orders and teaching orders of sisters, and of men also, derive from the Mother of Mercy. What a powerful impulse came to Dorothy Day, the radical and animating woman behind the Catholic Worker movement, from her devotion to Mary. Today this energy remains visible in the Mexican-American communities marching with a banner of Our Lady of Guadalupe in support of field-workers or of refugees from Central America. The prayer of the Church on her feast day taps into this energy.

> God of power and mercy, you blessed the Americas at Tepeyac with the presence of the virgin Mary of Guadalupe. May her prayers help all men and women to accept each other as brothers and sisters. Through your justice present in our hearts, may your peace reign in the world.

What should be clear after centuries of experience is that in the Catholic Church the love for what is sacramental – for fleshed-out signs of God's action – is always going to run the danger of getting overmaterialized. Attention that focuses on grandeur or quantity, on impressiveness, will risk missing the meaning. Jesus was aware of the problem. "Unless you see signs and wonders," he lamented to those who followed him, "you will not believe" (John 4:48). Many more people, apparently, are impressed by the awesome than are moved by the significant.

Yet amid excesses, the kernel of the genuine is right there, out in the open, available to all. Whatever apparitions and pieties develop around Mary, the best way to think about her, the truest form of devotion and connection, would still seem to be the prayer that constitutes her most abiding monument, the "Hail Mary." The "Hail Mary" is half praise and half petition. The praise is drawn right from the New Testament. She is the woman exceptionally "favored," or "graced"; she is included in the blessing that the Almighty extends over the holy one in her womb.

In the petition "Pray for us sinners now and at the hour of our death," which ends the Hail Mary, people recognize themselves as among God's poor, the *'anawim* of the psalms, asking her intervention. These words are still the most welcome and consoling that anyone can recite at the bedside of someone gravely ill. The Hail Mary, as a whole, fosters an attitude of humble reliance. With the phrase "among women" it also inculcates a quiet pride; you are very special, it says to Mary, among those who have not had power or occupied high standing but have nonetheless provided for human continuance. And among women whose dignity, gifts, and actions have gotten proper recognition, this "favor" of yours, so in tune with the Beatitudes, still acts as a guideline, an inspiration.

Something more needs filling in. Jesus himself, during his public ministry, heard some glowing praises directed toward his mother: "Blessed is the womb that bore you and the breasts that nursed you." He reacted by pointing out that Mary's holiness and dignity lay not principally in giving birth to him but in hearing God's word and doing it, in her readiness to be a faithful disciple. The concept of Mary as faithful disciple is strikingly, though simply, drawn in the miraculous image on the cloth at Guadalupe. But the other, complementary, concept of Mary as intercessor, medium of her son's grace, arms downward and outspread, is still popular and profound. In "The Church, the Goddess, and Mary" (unpublished), Ann Wittmann, S.C.S.C., a student of the figure of the Virgin Mary from feminist and many other perspectives, offers this helpful reminder:

> Although theologians of today call her the Mother of the Church and prefer to picture her as the *Ecclesia Orans,* hands chastely folded indicating her entire being is directed Godward, peasants and other common people, as Rosemary Ruether has remarked, prefer a kind of Earth Mother whose hands extend downwards in compassion and maternal goodness.

Over the centuries, while Catholic doctrine developed, and attention shifted across its various aspects, the figure of Mary has tended to attach itself, fit itself into, the figure of God caring for us human beings in Christ. The queenly images of the *Theotokos,* the God-bearer, evolved after the Council of Ephesus in 431, that moment in church history that so sharply affected all subsequent considerations of Mary. Ann Wittmann writes:

> As Christ's divinity became the focus of attention, so representations of Mary moved further and further from the portraits of her in the catacombs as a simple Roman matron. The ancient themes of the Magna Mater (Great Mother) were picked up and played in a multitude of variations. . . . This can be explained by the inadequacy of male images alone to reveal the total reality of God, and by the tendency or thrust that Fr. Andrew Greeley finds in human religions to search out symbols that reflect the femininity of God.

The search for this sort of symbol seems to be what Henry Adams (in *The Education of Henry Adams*) was considering when, astounded by the magnificence of the Cathedral of Chartres, he praised Our Lady in terms that seem to raise her above the divine son, much to the horror of Christian piety: "Symbol or energy, the Virgin had acted as the greatest force the Western world ever felt, and had drawn man's activities to herself more strongly than any other power, natural or supernatural, had ever done." What he is referring to, of course, is that burst of Marian piety, fired by St. Bernard, and the upsurge of confidence in the newly emerging towns that produced eighty cathedrals in France between the years 1100 and 1250, most of them dedicated to Notre Dame.

The church herself – *ecclesia, sponsa, sapientia, filia* – has always had to struggle to keep the image of Mary and devotion to Mary in focus. No story of a major Marian shrine – whether Lourdes, Guadalupe, Fatima, or any other – is complete without its episode of the local bishop, the apostolic teacher most responsible for the purity of Christian life, taking a long hard look at all the circumstances, testing affirmations and forms of piety in the light of the gospels as handed down, and trying to hold the reins on excess. The success of the bishop in testing and limiting and defining, when matched against the piety of the people, is far from a sure thing.

Vatican Council II was marked by dispute over the right way of presenting devotion to Our Lady. One pressure group held out for giving her a separate and special constitution. What prevailed, however, was the Council's delineation of Mary as inseparable from the mystery of the church; hence also the decision to include this within the "Constitution on the Church." Mary is to be integrated among the faithful; let there be no confusion of her with a goddess. Also, let all remember, draw fruit from, and perceive with sensitivity her maternal feelings and anxieties, her astonishment and puzzlement at God's ways, her openness and docility to them, her clouding over by the terrible darkness of her son's death, her companionship with the apostles.

Ann Wittmann concludes in line with the observations just expressed: "Mary may indeed be the key to wholeness in our perception of humanity." She it was, after all, who played and has continued to play the facilitating role in the history of the Incarnation.

REFLECTION AND ACTION

Food for Thought:

Marian devotion is a mark of Catholicity, and of ecumenical Christianity. Please specify how you stand with regard to it. Family life may have inculcated certain habits of piety; some bad tastes may linger with you; you may be aware of very special benefits and graces due to Mary's help.

Suggested Steps:

Practice a Marian inclusiveness in your religious life, honoring her aspects both of maternal intercessor and of faithful disciple.

Fear not to engage others in conversation about the role of Mary in Christian life and piety.

VIRGIN AND CHILD WITH SAINT ESTHER AND SAINT GIULIO

Hello, Mary, smiled upon,
God's with you, child-size
(though long since upraised)
for tendering of our awe.

The pick, you, among wise-woman
aunts, true hearts and lookers,
Sister our schoolyard pitcher –
the whole tribe of Esther.

Pick of your body's tree

too, a plan ripened, Jesus
looks trustingly at you,
before he's spurred on his way.

Maria, bent on God,
pray for us as for Saint Giulio,
our groundskeeper, pipe-smelly,
steady, though not much on church.

Whisper us each by name
to the small receiver
when achievement peels off
with a catch of the heart.

The discoveries that wait for us in a learned footnote! Rona
Goffen, in a long article about religious art in the fourteenth
century, alludes in tiny print, footnote 111, to "the 8th-cen-
tury practice of laying the Host of a Christmas Mass on a
crib that served as altar" ("*Nostra Conversatio in Caelis Est:
Observations on the *Sacra Conversazione* in the Trecento," in
Art Bulletin, June 1979, 198-222). What a marvel of the
Christian imagination! I had never heard of it before.

     Nativity scenes may date back a long way. Still, their
emergence as a staple of the Christmas season is owing to
Franciscan piety. One nativity celebration gave its impetus
to the myriad that would follow: the creche which St.
Francis lovingly designed for Christmas Mass at Greccio,
Italy, in 1223. Goffen quotes the Franciscan chronicler
Thomas of Celano: "Greccio was made, as it were, a new
Bethlehem. . . . A certain virtuous man saw a little child
lying in the manger lifeless, and he saw the holy man of
God [Francis] go up to it and rouse the child as from a deep
sleep."

     This "passionate veneration of God" elicited from Fran-
cis by images – what Goffen calls a "mingling of profound

reverence with a warm and human love" – became his legacy to later ages. It is palpable in the fourteenth-century manuscript *Meditations on the Life of Christ*, which encourages the reader, in prayer, to "pick the Child up and hold him in your arms. Gaze on his face with devotion and reverently kiss him and delight in him." Ignatius of Loyola, in the *Spiritual Exercises*, introducing the retreatant to the life of Christ through a contemplation of the nativity, instructs that person to savor every detail of the scene, even to put himself into it as a humble servant. Had not the Franciscan influence marked him?

Artists and sculptors in that era took their cue from Francis, delighting to recreate the Holy Family at this moment of the birth of Jesus, mostly in contemporary settings, often with the addition of shepherds and animals or exotic noblemen and their entourages. The scenes are among the favorites in European iconography.

Less well-known in art and piety is an infancy genre known as *sacra conversazione*, which thrived during the early and high Renaissance and then receded. The term, which dates from the early nineteenth century, is still used gingerly by art historians who argue about its application. The category itself originated in the era of Dante, circa 1300, when Pietro Lorenzetti decorated the Church of St. Francis at Assisi with a fresco in which the Madonna, holding the child, points to the stigmata displayed by St. Francis as a sign of what lay ahead for Jesus on his mission (an extraordinary reversal of time, although no more so than Francis's calling the child to life). Saint John the Evangelist stands to the other side, gesturing toward Jesus.

Sienese and related painters of the late Middle Ages, in other words, took to associating the saints with the Mother and Child. This increasingly vivid representation of the saints – often local persons who had lived in the recent past – was also a product of Franciscan piety, which

Goffen says had "an immense impact on the public imagination." Such figures not only stirred the faithful to imitation; they also offered themselves for recourse, as
intercessors with the Lord and his Mother. The Church of
St. Francis at Assisi set the pattern, according to Goffen:

> In the titular church of the Franciscan order early ex-
> amples appear which embody the spiritual and pictorial
> principles of *sacra conversazione*: the Mother and Child
> are united both physically and psychologically with the
> saints accompanying them, in a "holy community"
> joined together outside historical or narrative time and
> events.

Early artists of the Trecento – the Saint Nicholas Master, Simone Martini, disciples of Lorenzetti – tended to keep
the saints separated from Mother and Child by columns, or
arches, in self-contained areas of a painting. However formal
that may seem, these men were establishing a more intimate
mode than the late medieval *maestá*, a tableau of enthrone-
ment for the queenly Madonna with the royal infant on her
lap, surrounded by saints and angels, with members of the
faithful (often donors) kneeling in the foreground. In the
maestá, Mother and Child always appear disproportionately
large to denote their greater importance. The early masters
of the *sacra conversazione*, on the other hand, put all the
figures on one plane. Even while marking out divisions on
the canvas, they had the saints traverse them by glance and
gesture. Regarding *Five Franciscan Saints*, a painting by Simone Martini, Goffen says that despite the fact that the
saints are depicted in separate niches, "the exchanged
glances create the appearance of a discourse among
[them]."

In a small back chapel of St. John the Divine Cathedral
in New York City, the visitor will find a surprising retable –
a two-foot-high painting that stretches the length of the altar
rising just behind it. The artist? Giovanni di Paolo, of the

fifteenth century. Here in separate sections are Sts. Peter and Paul, ruggedly defined; an aging St. Andrew, with cross; a young John the Baptist – all in attitudes of communion with the Virgin and Child. This emphasis on interchange among the holy ones gradually led to a minimizing of separations; Lorenzetti, at the early date of his painting in Assisi, had already done without them.

Perhaps the most notable and full-scale example of the *sacra conversazione* is the Annalena Altarpiece by Fra Angelico, circa 1437. Here the artist skillfully groups well-known saints and sainted Dominicans attentive to one another and to the Mother and Child; all are in a sort of sanctuary. Arches are half indicated (at the top) and half masked. But some painters omitted the background details and thus set the scene timelessly in that otherworld, that other condition within our own world, which St. Paul referred to as the heavenly one. Andrea Mantegna does so in vivid color in *Virgin and Child with St. John and Other Saints,* now in the Sabauda Gallery of Turin, Italy.

The term *sacra conversazione* was not really intended to designate a paradise in which the saints converse with Our Lord and Our Lady (though Fra Angelico and others did love to imagine this scene); it arose as a comment on the holy life to which all the faithful on earth are called by grace. The phrase is an allusion to St. Paul telling the Philippians, *"Nostra conversatio in caelis est"* in St. Jerome's Latin version of the Greek (called "the Vulgate"). How to put this in English? Perhaps "Our way of living is in heaven." St. Paul had used the Greek *politeuma,* meaning citizenship, or life as citizens, as if to say "Our civic life is in heaven." Jerome more than once translated this Greek word (among others) from Paul by the Latin verb *conversari* (to carry on one's life) – not just to talk or to converse (as we now translate the term) but to live in a milieu together. How difficult to carry over shadings from one language to another!

To reflect, then, on this lovely genre: the Christmas cards we see that may strike us as abstract because, rather than showing a manger scene, they depict the Virgin and Child with a saint or two, are actually inviting us into that space. They are introducing us to the nascent Lord at his most fragile and incipient, and to his intercessor-mother as the guarantee of his humanness. Saintly fellow humans, members of our community as well as of theirs, give us assurance, invite us to believe and trust in the Incarnate One.

How we wish more of these depictions of the *sacra conversazione* would be contemporary with ourselves. How we would like to see figures whom we can recognize – Dorothy Day, Maximilian Kolbe, Pope John XXIII, Sister Thea Bowman – figures in garb familiar to us, with gestures natural to us as well as to them. Then we would get the idea. Then we would enter into the mystery more and more each year with the return of this feast of Christ's beginning. "Now we too can begin to be Christian" – that's what we should be impelled to say when we see greeting cards that invite us toward the *sacra conversazione*.

REFLECTION AND ACTION

Food for Thought:

An "otherworld condition" can be constituted in our earthly world by holy conversation, or familiarity, with favorite saints – always, to be sure, grouped around Jesus Christ. Ponder in what terms you may have been able to realize this. Hint: The saints in my poem start with St. Mary, of highest esteem and role, and include some women named Esther who much affected me (a favorite aunt, a favorite grade-school teacher, an impressive young woman in a Mexican village), plus an Italian gardener to whom I was attached, growing up by the name of Giulio.

Suggested Steps:

Begin or continue to try realizing this condition of *sacra conversazione.*

CONCLUSION

REACHING: A SONG

I won't swell out for a medal
or contentedly fold my arms.
I'm still unfinished and partial
still reaching toward you.

Refrain:
Like a tendril up and up I go
to the source of light.
Like an infant I will reach and reach
to the clasp of life.

Can't let the world and its worries
succeed in pinning my arms.
I'm alive on a greener prairie
stretching toward you.

No failure flatten my ego
or get me drooping my arms.
I'm called to the saints as equal
setting sights on you.

If a gap seems to open wider
between you and my own poor arms,
dear goal of our sighs, remind me
I'm touching on you.